ACRES OF DIAMONDS

ACRES
OF DIAMONDS

BY

RUSSELL H. CONWELL

FOUNDER OF TEMPLE UNIVERSITY
PHILADELPHIA

WITH AN AUTOBIOGRAPHICAL NOTE

SUN BOOKS
Sun Publishing Company

Acres of Diamonds

First Sun Books Printing --- 2005

This Edition Copyright © 2005 by
Sun Publishing Company

Sun Books
are published by
Sun Publishing Company
PO Box 5588, Santa Fe
NM 87502-5588 USA

www.SunBooks.com

ISBN: 0-89540-418-4

ACRES OF DIAMONDS

Copyright, 1915, by Harper & Brothers
Printed in the United States of America

M-A

Russell H. Conwell

CONTENTS

AN APPRECIATION

THOUGH Russell H. Conwell's Acres of Diamonds have been spread all over the United States, time and care have made them more valuable, and now that they have been reset in black and white by their discoverer, they are to be laid in the hands of a multitude for their enrichment.

In the same case with these gems there is a fascinating story of the Master Jeweler's life-work which splendidly illustrates the ultimate unit of power by showing what one man can do in one day and what one life is worth to the world.

As his neighbor and intimate friend in Philadelphia for thirty years, I am free to say that Russell H. Conwell's tall, manly figure stands out in the state of Pennsylvania as its first citizen and "The Big Brother" of its seven millions of people.

From the beginning of his career he has been a credible witness in the Court of Public Works to the truth of the strong language of the New Testament Parable where it says, "If ye have faith as a grain of mustard-seed, ye shall say unto this mountain, 'Remove hence to yonder place,' AND IT SHALL REMOVE AND NOTHING SHALL BE IMPOSSIBLE UNTO YOU."

As a student, schoolmaster, lawyer, preacher, organizer, thinker and writer, lecturer, educator, diplomat, and leader of men, he has made his mark on his city and state and the times in which he has lived. A man dies, but his good work lives.

His ideas, ideals, and enthusiasms have inspired tens of thousands of lives. A book full of the energetics of a master workman is just what every young man cares for.

1915.

His yoke fellow

John Wanamaker

Friends.—This lecture has been delivered under these circumstances: I visit a town or city, and try to arrive there early
enough to see the postmaster, the barber, the keeper of the hotel,
the principal of the schools, and the ministers of some of the
churches, and then go into some of the factories and stores, and
talk with the people, and get into sympathy with the local conditions of that town or city and see what has been their history,
what opportunities they had, and what they had failed to do—
and every town fails to do something—and then go to the lecture
and talk to those people about the subjects which applied to
their locality. "Acres of Diamonds"—the idea—has continu-
ously been precisely the same. The idea is that in this country
of ours every man has the opportunity to make more of himself
than he does in his own environment, with his own skill, with
his own energy, and with his own friends.

RUSSELL H. CONWELL.

ACRES OF DIAMONDS

ACRES OF DIAMONDS

WHEN going down the Tigris and Euphrates rivers many years ago with a party of English travelers I found myself under the direction of an old Arab guide whom we hired up at Bagdad, and I have often thought how that guide resembled our barbers in certain mental characteristics. He thought that it was not only his duty to guide us down those rivers, and do what he was paid for doing, but also to entertain us with stories curious and weird, ancient and modern, strange and familiar. Many of them I have forgotten, and I am glad I have, but there is one I shall never forget.

The old guide was leading my camel by its halter along the banks of those ancient rivers, and he told me story after story until I grew weary

---

This is the most recent and complete form of the lecture. It happened to be delivered in Philadelphia, Dr. Conwell's home city. When he says "right here in Philadelphia," he means the home city, town, or village of every reader of this book, just as he would use the name of it if delivering the lecture there, instead of doing it through the pages which follow.

of his story-telling and ceased to listen. I have never been irritated with that guide when he lost his temper as I ceased listening. But I remember that he took off his Turkish cap and swung it in a circle to get my attention. I could see it through the corner of my eye, but I determined not to look straight at him for fear he would tell another story. But although I am not a woman, I did finally look, and as soon as I did he went right into another story.

Said he, "I will tell you a story now which I reserve for my particular friends." When he emphasized the words "particular friends," I listened, and I have ever been glad I did. I really feel devoutly thankful, that there are 1,674 young men who have been carried through college by this lecture who are also glad that I did listen. The old guide told me that there once lived not far from the River Indus an ancient Persian by the name of Ali Hafed. He said that Ali Hafed owned a very large farm, that he had orchards, grain-fields, and gardens; that he had money at interest, and was a wealthy and contented man. He was contented because he was wealthy, and wealthy because he was contented. One day there visited that old Persian farmer one of those ancient Buddhist priests, one of the wise men of the East. He sat down by the fire and told the old farmer how this world of ours was made. He said that this world was once a mere bank of fog, and that the Almighty thrust His finger into

ACRES OF DIAMONDS

this bank of fog, and began slowly to move His
finger around, increasing the speed until at last
He whirled this bank of fog into a solid ball of
fire. Then it went rolling through the universe,
burning its way through other banks of fog, and
condensed the moisture without, until it fell in
floods of rain upon its hot surface, and cooled
the outward crust. Then the internal fires bursting outward through the crust threw up the mountains and hills, the valleys, the plains and prairies
of this wonderful world of ours. If this internal
molten mass came bursting out and cooled very
quickly it became granite; less quickly copper,
less quickly silver, less quickly gold, and, after
gold, diamonds were made.

Said the old priest, "A diamond is a congealed
drop of sunlight." Now that is literally scien-
tifically true, that a diamond is an actual deposit
of carbon from the sun. The old priest told Ali
Hafed that if he had one diamond the size of
his thumb he could purchase the county, and if
he had a mine of diamonds he could place his
children upon thrones through the influence of
their great wealth.

Ali Hafed heard all about diamonds, how much
they were worth, and went to his bed that night
a poor man. He had not lost anything, but he
was poor because he was discontented, and discontented because he feared he was poor. He
said, "I want a mine of diamonds," and he lay
awake all night.

5

ACRES OF DIAMONDS

Early in the morning he sought out the priest. I know by experience that a priest is very cross when awakened early in the morning, and when he shook that old priest out of his dreams, Ali Hafed said to him:

"Will you tell me where I can find diamonds?"

"Diamonds! What do you want with diamonds?" "Why, I wish to be immensely rich." "Well, then, go along and find them. That is all you have to do; go and find them, and then you have them." "But I don't know where to go." "Well, if you will find a river that runs through white sands, between high mountains, in those white sands you will always find diamonds." "I don't believe there is any such river." "Oh yes, there are plenty of them. All you have to do is to go and find them, and then you have them." Said Ali Hafed, "I will go."

So he sold his farm, collected his money, left his family in charge of a neighbor, and away he went in search of diamonds. He began his search, very properly to my mind, at the Mountains of the Moon. Afterward he came around into Palestine, then wandered on into Europe, and at last when his money was all spent and he was in rags, wretchedness, and poverty, he stood on the shore of that bay at Barcelona, in Spain, when a great tidal wave came rolling in between the pillars of Hercules, and the poor, afflicted, suffering, dying man could not resist the awful temptation to cast himself into that incoming tide, and he sank beneath its foaming crest, never to rise in this life again.

When that old guide had told me that awfully sad story he stopped the camel I was riding on and went back to fix the baggage that was coming off another camel, and I had an opportunity to muse over his story while he was gone. I remember saying to myself, "Why did he reserve that story for his 'particular friends'?" There seemed to be no beginning, no middle, no end, nothing to it. That was the first story I had ever heard told in my life, and would be the first one I ever read, in which the hero was killed in the first chapter. I had but one chapter of that story, and the hero was dead.

When the guide came back and took up the halter of my camel, he went right ahead with the story, into the second chapter, just as though there had been no break. The man who purchased Ali Hafed's farm one day led his camel into the garden to drink, and as that camel put its nose into the shallow water of that garden brook, Ali Hafed's successor noticed a curious flash of light from the white sands of the stream. He pulled out a black stone having an eye of light reflecting all the hues of the rainbow. He took the pebble into the house and put it on the mantel which covers the central fires, and forgot all about it.

A few days later this same old priest came in to visit Ali Hafed's successor, and the moment

he opened that drawing-room door he saw that
flash of light on the mantel, and he rushed up
to it, and shouted: "Here is a diamond! Has Ali
Hafed returned?" "Oh no, Ali Hafed has not returned, and that is not a diamond. That is nothing but a stone we found right out here in our
own garden." "But," said the priest, "I tell you
I know a diamond when I see it. I know posi-
tively that is a diamond."

Then together they rushed out into that old
garden and stirred up the white sands with their
fingers, and lo! there came up other more beautiful and valuable gems than the first. "Thus,"
said the guide to me, and, friends, it is historically
true, "was discovered the diamond-mine of Golconda, the most magnificent diamond-mine in
all the history of mankind, excelling the Kimberly
itself. The Kohinoor, and the Orloff of the crown
jewels of England and Russia, the largest on earth,
came from that mine."

When that old Arab guide told me the second
chapter of his story, he then took off his Turkish
cap and swung it around in the air again to get
my attention to the moral. Those Arab guides
have morals to their stories, although they are
not always moral. As he swung his hat, he said
to me, "Had Ali Hafed remained at home and dug
in his own cellar, or underneath his own wheat-
fields, or in his own garden, instead of wretchedness, starvation, and death by suicide in a strange
land, he would have had 'acres of diamonds.'

ACRES OF DIAMONDS

For every acre of that old farm, yes, every shovelful, afterward revealed gems which since have decorated the crowns of monarchs."

When he had added the moral to his story I saw why he reserved it for "his particular friends." But I did not tell him I could see it. It was that mean old Arab's way of going around a thing like a lawyer, to say indirectly what he did not dare say directly, that "in his private opinion there was a certain young man then traveling down the Tigris River that might better be at home in America." I did not tell him I could see that, but I told him his story reminded me of one, and I told it to him quick, and I think I will tell it to you.

I told him of a man out in California in 1847, who owned a ranch. He heard they had discovered gold in southern California, and so with a passion for gold he sold his ranch to Colonel Sutter, and away he went, never to come back. Colonel Sutter put a mill upon a stream that ran through that ranch, and one day his little girl brought some wet sand from the raceway into their home and sifted it through her fingers before the fire, and in that falling sand a visitor saw the first shining scales of real gold that were ever discovered in California. The man who had owned that ranch wanted gold, and he could have secured it for the mere taking. Indeed, thirty-eight millions of dollars has been taken out of a very few acres since then. About eight years ago I delivered this lecture in a city that stands on that farm, and they told me that a one-third owner for years and years had been getting one hundred and twenty dollars in gold every fifteen minutes, sleeping or waking, without taxation. You and I would enjoy an income like that—if we didn't have to pay an income tax.

But a better illustration really than that occurred here in our own Pennsylvania. If there is anything I enjoy above another on the platform, it is to get one of these German audiences in Pennsylvania before me, and fire that at them, and I enjoy it to-night. There was a man living in Pennsylvania, not unlike some Pennsylvanians you have seen, who owned a farm, and he did with that farm just what I should do with a farm if I owned one in Pennsylvania—he sold it. But before he sold it he decided to secure employment collecting coal-oil for his cousin, who was in the business in Canada, where they first discovered oil on this continent. They dipped it from the running streams at that early time. So this Pennsylvania farmer wrote to his cousin asking for employment. You see, friends, this farmer was not altogether a foolish man. No, he was not. He did not leave his farm until he had something else to do. *Of all the simpletons the stars shine on I don't know of a worse one than the man who leaves one job before he has gotten another.* That has especial reference to my profession, and has no reference whatever to a man

ACRES OF DIAMONDS

seeking a divorce. When he wrote to his cousin for employment, his cousin replied, "I cannot engage you because you know nothing about the oil business."

Well, then the old farmer said, "I will know," and with most commendable zeal (characteristic of the students of Temple University) he set himself at the study of the whole subject. He began away back at the second day of God's creation when this world was covered thick and deep with that rich vegetation which since has turned to the primitive beds of coal. He studied the subject until he found that the drainings really of those rich beds of coal furnished the coal-oil that was worth pumping, and then he found how it came up with the living springs. He studied until he knew what it looked like, smelled like, tasted like, and how to refine it. Now said he in his letter to his cousin, "I understand the oil business." His cousin answered, "All right, come on."

So he sold his farm, according to the county record, for $833 (even money, "no cents"). He had scarcely gone from that place before the man who purchased the spot went out to arrange for the watering of the cattle. He found the previous owner had gone out years before and put a plank across the brook back of the barn, edgewise into the surface of the water just a few inches. The purpose of that plank at that sharp angle across the brook was to throw over to the other bank a dreadful-looking scum through which the cattle would not put their noses. But with that plank there to throw it all over to one side, the cattle would drink below, and thus that man who had gone to Canada had been himself damming back for twenty-three years a flood of coal-oil which the state geologists of Pennsylvania declared to us ten years later was even then worth a hundred millions of dollars to our state, and four years ago our geologist declared the discovery to be worth to our state a thousand millions of dollars. The man who owned that territory on which the city of Titusville now stands, and those Pleasantville valleys, had studied the subject from the second day of God's creation clear down to the present time. He studied it until he knew all about it, and yet he is said to have sold the whole of it for $833, and again I say, "no sense."

But I need another illustration. I found it in Massachusetts, and I am sorry I did because that is the state I came from. This young man in Massachusetts furnishes just another phase of my thought. He went to Yale College and studied mines and mining, and became such an adept as a mining engineer that he was employed by the authorities of the university to train students who were behind their classes. During his senior year he earned $15 a week for doing that work. When he graduated they raised his pay from $15 to $45 a week, and offered him a professorship, and as soon as they did he went right home to his mother.

ACRES OF DIAMONDS

If they had raised that boy's pay from $15 to $15.60
he would have stayed and been proud of the place,
but when they put it up to $45 at one leap, he said,
"Mother, I won't work for $45 a week. The idea
of a man with a brain like mine working for $45
a week! Let's go out in California and stake out
gold-mines and silver-mines, and be immensely
rich."

Said his mother, "Now, Charlie, it is just as
well to be happy as it is to be rich."

"Yes," said Charlie, "but it is just as well to
be rich and happy, too." And they were both
right about it. As he was an only son and
she a widow, of course he had his way. They
always do.

They sold out in Massachusetts, and instead
of going to California they went to Wisconsin,
where he went into the employ of the Superior
Copper Mining Company at $15 a week again,
but with the proviso in his contract that he should
have an interest in any mines he should discover
for the company. I don't believe he ever discovered a mine, and if I am looking in the face of any
stockholder of that copper company you wish
he had discovered something or other. I have
friends who are not here because they could not
afford a ticket, who did have stock in that company at the time this young man was employed
there. This young man went out there, and I
have not heard a word from him. I don't know
what became of him, and I don't know whether

he found any mines or not, but I don't believe he ever did.

But I do know the other end of the line. He had scarcely gotten out of the old homestead before the succeeding owner went out to dig potatoes. The potatoes were already growing in the ground when he bought the farm, and as the old farmer was bringing in a basket of potatoes it hugged very tight between the ends of the stone fence. You know in Massachusetts our farms are nearly all stone wall. There you are obliged to be very economical of front gateways in order to have some place to put the stone. When that basket hugged so tight he set it down on the ground, and then dragged on one side, and pulled on the other side, and as he was dragging that basket through this farmer noticed in the upper and outer corner of that stone wall, right next the gate, a block of native silver eight inches square. That professor of mines, mining, and mineralogy who knew so much about the subject that he would not work for $45 a week, when he sold that homestead in Massachusetts sat right on that silver to make the bargain. He was born on that homestead, was brought up there, and had gone back and forth rubbing the stone with his sleeve until it reflected his countenance, and seemed to say, "Here is a hundred thousand dollars right down here just for the taking." But he would not take it. It was in a home in Newburyport, Massachusetts, and there was no silver there, all away off—well, I don't know where, and he did not, but somewhere else, and he was a professor of mineralogy.

My friends, that mistake is very universally made, and why should we even smile at him. I often wonder what has become of him. I do not know at all, but I will tell you what I "guess" as a Yankee. I guess that he sits out there by his fireside to-night with his friends gathered around him, and he is saying to them something like this: "Do you know that man Conwell who lives in Philadelphia?" "Oh yes, I have heard of him." "Do you know that man Jones that lives in Philadelphia?" "Yes, I have heard of him, too."

Then he begins to laugh, and shakes his sides, and says to his friends, "Well, they have done just the same thing I did, precisely"—and that spoils the whole joke, for you and I have done the same thing he did, and while we sit here and laugh at him he has a better right to sit out there and laugh at us. I know I have made the same mistakes, but, of course, that does not make any difference, because we don't expect the same man to preach and practise, too.

As I come here to-night and look around this audience I am seeing again what through these fifty years I have continually seen—men that are making precisely that same mistake. I often wish I could see the younger people, and would that the Academy had been filled to-night with our high-school scholars and our grammar-school scholars,

that I could have them to talk to. While I would
have preferred such an audience as that, because
they are most susceptible, as they have not grown
up into their prejudices as we have, they have
not gotten into any custom that they cannot
break, they have not met with any failures as
we have; and while I could perhaps do such an
audience as that more good than I can do grown-
up people, yet I will do the best I can with the
material I have. I say to you that you have
"acres of diamonds" in Philadelphia right where
you now live. "Oh," but you will say, "you
cannot know much about your city if you think
there are any 'acres of diamonds' here."

I was greatly interested in that account in the
newspaper of the young man who found that
diamond in North Carolina. It was one of the
purest diamonds that has ever been discovered,
and it has several predecessors near the same
locality. I went to a distinguished professor in
mineralogy and asked him where he thought those
diamonds came from. The professor secured the
map of the geologic formations of our continent,
and traced it. He said it went either through the
underlying carboniferous strata adapted for such
production, westward through Ohio and the Mis-
sissippi, or in more probability came eastward
through Virginia and up the shore of the Atlantic
Ocean. It is a fact that the diamonds were there,
for they have been discovered and sold; and that
they were carried down there during the drift

period, from some northern locality. Now who
can say but some person going down with his
drill in Philadelphia will find some trace of a diamond-mine yet down here? Oh, friends! you cannot say that you are not over one of the greatest
diamond-mines in the world, for such a diamond
as that only comes from the most profitable mines
that are found on earth.

But it serves simply to illustrate my thought,
which I emphasize by saying if you do not have
the actual diamond-mines literally you have all
that they would be good for to you. Because
now that the Queen of England has given the
greatest compliment ever conferred upon American
woman for her attire because she did not appear
with any jewels at all at the late reception in
England, it has almost done away with the use
of diamonds anyhow. All you would care for
would be the few you would wear if you wish
to be modest, and the rest you would sell for
money.

Now then, I say again that the opportunity
to get rich, to attain unto great wealth, is here
in Philadelphia now, within the reach of almost
every man and woman who hears me speak to-
night, and I mean just what I say. I have not
come to this platform even under these circumstances to recite something to you. I have come
to tell you what in God's sight I believe to be the
truth, and if the years of life have been of any
value to me in the attainment of common sense,

ACRES OF DIAMONDS

I know I am right; that the men and women sitting here, who found it difficult perhaps to buy a ticket to this lecture or gathering to-night, have within their reach "acres of diamonds," opportunities to get largely wealthy. There never was a place on earth more adapted than the city of Philadelphia to-day, and never in the history of the world did a poor man without capital have such an opportunity to get rich quickly and honestly as he has now in our city. I say it is the truth, and I want you to accept it as such; for if you think I have come to simply recite something, then I would better not be here. I have no time to waste in any such talk, but to say the things I believe, and unless some of you get richer for what I am saying to-night my time is wasted.

I say that you ought to get rich, and it is your duty to get rich. How many of my pious brethren say to me, "Do you, a Christian minister, spend your time going up and down the country advising young people to get rich, to get money?" "Yes, of course I do." They say, "Isn't that awful! Why don't you preach the gospel instead of preaching about man's making money?" "Because to make money honestly is to preach the gospel." That is the reason. The men who get rich may be the most honest men you find in the community.

"Oh," but says some young man here to-night, "I have been told all my life that if a person has money he is very dishonest and dishonorable and mean and contemptible." My friend, that is the reason why you have none, because you have that idea of people. The foundation of your faith is altogether false. Let me say here clearly, and say it briefly, though subject to discussion which I have not time for here, ninety-eight out of one hundred of the rich men of America are honest. That is why they are rich. That is why they are trusted with money. That is why they carry on great enterprises and find plenty of people to work with them. It is because they are honest men.

Says another young man, "I hear sometimes of men that get millions of dollars dishonestly." Yes, of course you do, and so do I. But they are so rare a thing in fact that the newspapers talk about them all the time as a matter of news until you get the idea that all the other rich men got rich dishonestly.

My friend, you take and drive me—if you furnish the auto—out into the suburbs of Philadelphia, and introduce me to the people who own their homes around this great city, those beautiful homes with gardens and flowers, those magnificent homes so lovely in their art, and I will introduce you to the very best people in character as well as in enterprise in our city, and you know I will. A man is not really a true man until he owns his own home, and they that own their homes are made more honorable and honest and pure, and true and economical and careful, by owning the home.

For a man to have money, even in large sums, is not an inconsistent thing. We preach against covetousness, and you know we do, in the pulpit, and oftentimes preach against it so long and use the terms about "filthy lucre" so extremely that Christians get the idea that when we stand in the pulpit we believe it is wicked for any man to have money—until the collection-basket goes around, and then we almost swear at the people because they don't give more money. Oh, the inconsistency of such doctrines as that!

Money is power, and you ought to be reasonably ambitious to have it. You ought because you can do more good with it than you could without it. Money printed your Bible, money builds your churches, money sends your missionaries, and money pays your preachers, and you would not have many of them, either, if you did not pay them. I am always willing that my church should raise my salary, because the church that pays the largest salary always raises it the easiest. You never knew an exception to it in your life. The man who gets the largest salary can do the most good with the power that is furnished to him. Of course he can if his spirit be right to use it for what it is given to him.

I say, then, you ought to have money. If you can honestly attain unto riches in Philadelphia, it is your Christian and godly duty to do so.

ACRES OF DIAMONDS

It is an awful mistake of these pious people to think you must be awfully poor in order to be pious.

Some men say, "Don't you sympathize with the poor people?" Of course I do, or else I would not have been lecturing these years. I won't give in but what I sympathize with the poor, but the number of poor who are to be sympathized with is very small. To sympathize with a man whom God has punished for his sins, thus to help him when God would still continue a just punishment, is to do wrong, no doubt about it, and we do that more than we help those who are deserving. While we should sympathize with God's poor—that is, those who cannot help themselves— let us remember there is not a poor person in the United States who was not made poor by his own shortcomings, or by the shortcomings of some one else. It is all wrong to be poor, anyhow. Let us give in to that argument and pass that to one side.

A gentleman gets up back there, and says, "Don't you think there are some things in this world that are better than money?" Of course I do, but I am talking about money now. Of course there are some things higher than money. Oh yes, I know by the grave that has left me standing alone that there are some things in this world that are higher and sweeter and purer than money. Well do I know there are some things higher and grander than gold. Love is the grandest thing on God's earth, but fortunate the lover who has plenty of money. Money is power, money is force, money will do good as well as harm. In the hands of good men and women it could accomplish, and it has accomplished, good.

I hate to leave that behind me. I heard a man get up in a prayer-meeting in our city and thank the Lord he was "one of God's poor." Well, I wonder what his wife thinks about that? She earns all the money that comes into that house, and he smokes a part of that on the veranda. I don't want to see any more of the Lord's poor of that kind, and I don't believe the Lord does. And yet there are some people who think in order to be pious you must be awfully poor and awfully dirty. That does not follow at all. While we sympathize with the poor, let us not teach a doctrine like that.

Yet the age is prejudiced against advising a Christian man (or, as a Jew would say, a godly man) from attaining unto wealth. The prejudice is so universal and the years are far enough back, I think, for me to safely mention that years ago up at Temple University there was a young man in our theological school who thought he was the only pious student in that department. He came into my office one evening and sat down by my desk, and said to me: "Mr. President, I think it is my duty sir, to come in and labor with you." "What has happened now?" Said he, "I heard you say at the Academy, at the Peirce School commencement, that you thought it was an honorable ambition for a young man to desire to have wealth, and that you thought it made him temperate, made him anxious to have a good name, and made him industrious. You spoke about man's ambition to have money helping to make him a good man. Sir, I have come to tell you the Holy Bible says that 'money is the root of all evil.'"

I told him I had never seen it in the Bible, and advised him to go out into the chapel and get the Bible, and show me the place. So out he went for the Bible, and soon he stalked into my office with the Bible open, with all the bigoted pride of the narrow sectarian, or of one who founds his Christianity on some misinterpretation of Scripture. He flung the Bible down on my desk, and fairly squealed into my ear: "There it is, Mr. President; you can read it for yourself." I said to him: "Well, young man, you will learn when you get a little older that you cannot trust another denomination to read the Bible for you. You belong to another denomination. You are taught in the theological school, however, that emphasis is exegesis. Now, will you take that Bible and read it yourself, and give the proper emphasis to it?"

He took the Bible, and proudly read, "'The love of money is the root of all evil.'"

Then he had it right, and when one does quote aright from that same old Book he quotes the absolute truth. I have lived through fifty years of the mightiest battle that old Book has ever fought, and I have lived to see its banners flying

3 23

free; for never in the history of this world did the great minds of earth so universally agree that the Bible is true—all true—as they do at this very hour.

So I say that when he quoted right, of course he quoted the absolute truth. "The love of money is the root of all evil." He who tries to attain unto it too quickly, or dishonestly, will fall into many snares, no doubt about that. The love of money. What is that? It is making an idol of money, and idolatry pure and simple everywhere is condemned by the Holy Scriptures and by man's common sense. The man that worships the dollar instead of thinking of the purposes for which it ought to be used, the man who idolizes simply money, the miser that hordes his money in the cellar, or hides it in his stocking, or refuses to invest it where it will do the world good, that man who hugs the dollar until the eagle squeals has in him the root of all evil.

I think I will leave that behind me now and answer the question of nearly all of you who are asking, "Is there opportunity to get rich in Philadelphia?" Well, now, how simple a thing it is to see where it is, and the instant you see where it is it is yours. Some old gentleman gets up back there and says, "Mr. Conwell, have you lived in Philadelphia for thirty-one years and don't know that the time has gone by when you can make anything in this city?" "No, I don't think it is." "Yes, it is; I have tried it." "What business are you in?" "I kept a store here for twenty years, and never made over a thousand dollars in the whole twenty years."

"Well, then, you can measure the good you have been to this city by what this city has paid you, because a man can judge very well what he is worth by what he receives; that is, in what he is to the world at this time. If you have not made over a thousand dollars in twenty years in Philadelphia, it would have been better for Philadelphia if they had kicked you out of the city nineteen years and nine months ago. A man has no right to keep a store in Philadelphia twenty years and not make at least five hundred thousand dollars, even though it be a corner grocery up-town." You say, "You cannot make five thousand dollars in a store now." Oh, my friends, if you will just take only four blocks around you, and find out what the people want and what you ought to supply and set them down with your pencil, and figure up the profits you would make if you did supply them, you would very soon see it. There is wealth right within the sound of your voice.

Some one says: "You don't know anything about business. A preacher never knows a thing about business." Well, then, I will have to prove that I am an expert. I don't like to do this, but I have to do it because my testimony will not be taken if I am not an expert. My father kept a country store, and if there is any place under the stars where a man gets all sorts of experience in every kind of mercantile transactions, it is in the country store. I am not proud of my experience, but sometimes when my father was away he would leave me in charge of the store, though fortunately for him that was not very often. But this did occur many times, friends: A man would come in the store, and say to me, "Do you keep jack-knives?" "No, we don't keep jack-knives," and I went off whistling a tune. What did I care about that man, anyhow? Then another farmer would come in and say, "Do you keep jack-knives?" "No, we don't keep jack-knives." Then I went away and whistled another tune. Then a third man came right in the same door and said, "Do you keep jack-knives?" "No. Why is every one around here asking for jack-knives? Do you suppose we are keeping this store to supply the whole neighborhood with jack-knives?" Do you carry on your store like that in Philadelphia? The difficulty was I had not then learned that the foundation of godliness and the foundation principle of success in business are both the same precisely. The man who says, "I cannot carry my religion into business" advertises himself either as being an imbecile in business, or on the road to bankruptcy, or a thief, one of the three, sure. He will fail within a very few years. He certainly will if he doesn't carry his religion into business. If I had been carrying on my father's store on a Christian plan, godly plan, I would have had a jack-knife for the third man when he called for it. Then I would have actually done him a kindness, and I would have received a reward myself, which it would have been my duty to take.

There are some over-pious Christian people who think if you take any profit on anything you sell that you are an unrighteous man. On the contrary, you would be a criminal to sell goods for less than they cost. You have no right to do that. You cannot trust a man with your money who cannot take care of his own. You cannot trust a man in your family that is not true to his own wife. You cannot trust a man in the world that does not begin with his own heart, his own character, and his own life. It would have been my duty to have furnished a jack-knife to the third man, or the second, and to have sold it to him and actually profited myself. I have no more right to sell goods without making a profit on them than I have to overcharge him dishonestly beyond what they are worth. But I should so sell each bill of goods that the person to whom I sell shall make as much as I make.

To live and let live is the principle of the gospel, and the principle of every-day common sense. Oh, young man, hear me; live as you go along. Do not wait until you have reached my years before you begin to enjoy anything of this life. If I had the millions back, or fifty cents of it, which I have tried to earn in these years, it would not do me anything like the good that it does me now in this almost sacred presence to-night. Oh, yes, I am paid over and over a hundredfold to-night for dividing as I have tried to do in some measure as I went along through the years. I ought not speak that way, it sounds egotistic, but I am old enough now to be excused for that. I should have helped my fellow-men, which I have tried to do, and every one should try to do, and get the happiness of it. The man who goes home with the sense that he has stolen a dollar that day, that he has robbed a man of what was his honest due, is not going to sweet rest. He arises tired in the morning, and goes with an unclean conscience to his work the next day. He is not a successful man at all, although he may have laid up millions. But the man who has gone through life dividing always with his fellow-men, making and demanding his own rights and his own profits, and giving to every other man his rights and profits, lives every day, and not only that, but it is the royal road to great wealth. The history of the thousands of millionaires shows that to be the case.

The man over there who said he could not make anything in a store in Philadelphia has been carrying on his store on the wrong principle. Suppose I go into your store to-morrow morning and ask, "Do you know neighbor A, who lives one square away, at house No. 1240?" "Oh yes, I have met him. He deals here at the corner store." "Where did he come from?" "I don't know." "How many does he have in his family?" "I don't know." "What ticket does he vote?" "I don't know." "What church does he go to?" "I don't know, and don't care. What are you asking all these questions for?"

If you had a store in Philadelphia would you answer me like that? If so, then you are conducting your business just as I carried on my father's business in Worthington, Massachusetts. You don't know where your neighbor came from when he moved to Philadelphia, and you don't care. If you had cared you would be a rich man now. If you had cared enough about him to take an interest in his affairs, to find out what he needed, you would have been rich. But you go through the world saying, "No opportunity to get rich," and there is the fault right at your own door.

But another young man gets up over there and says, "I cannot take up the mercantile business." (While I am talking of trade it applies to every occupation.) "Why can't you go into the mercantile business?" "Because I haven't any capital." Oh, the weak and dudish creature that can't see over its collar! It makes a person weak to see these little dudes standing around the corners and saying, "Oh, if I had plenty of capital, how rich I would get." "Young man, do you think you are going to get rich on capital?" "Certainly." Well, I say, "Certainly not." If your mother has plenty of money, and she will

29

set you up in business, you will "set her up in business," supplying you with capital.

The moment a young man or woman gets more money than he or she has grown to by practical experience, that moment he has gotten a curse. It is no help to a young man or woman to inherit money. It is no help to your children to leave them money, but if you leave them education, if you leave them Christian and noble character, if you leave them a wide circle of friends, if you leave them an honorable name, it is far better than that they should have money. It would be worse for them, worse for the nation, that they should have any money at all. Oh, young man, if you have inherited money, don't regard it as a help. It will curse you through your years, and deprive you of the very best things of human life. There is no class of people to be pitied so much as the inexperienced sons and daughters of the rich of our generation. I pity the rich man's son. He can never know the best things in life.

One of the best things in our life is when a young man has earned his own living, and when he becomes engaged to some lovely young woman, and makes up his mind to have a home of his own. Then with that same love comes also that divine inspiration toward better things, and he begins to save his money. He begins to leave off his bad habits and put money in the bank. When he has a few hundred dollars he goes out in the suburbs to look for a home. He goes to the savings-bank, perhaps, for half of the value, and then goes for his wife, and when he takes his bride over the threshold of that door for the first time he says in words of eloquence my voice can never touch: "I have earned this home myself. It is all mine, and I divide with thee." That is the grandest moment a human heart may ever know.

But a rich man's son can never know that. He takes his bride into a finer mansion, it may be, but he is obliged to go all the way through it and say to his wife, "My mother gave me that, my mother gave me that, and my mother gave me this," until his wife wishes she had married his mother. I pity the rich man's son.

The statistics of Massachusetts showed that not one rich man's son out of seventeen ever dies rich. I pity the rich man's sons unless they have the good sense of the elder Vanderbilt, which sometimes happens. He went to his father and said, "Did you earn all your money?" "I did, my son. I began to work on a ferry-boat for twenty-five cents a day." "Then," said his son, "I will have none of your money," and he, too, tried to get employment on a ferry-boat that Saturday night. He could not get one there, but he did get a place for three dollars a week. Of course, if a rich man's son will do that, he will get the discipline of a poor boy that is worth more than a university education to any man. He would then be able to take care of the millions of his father. But as a rule the

ACRES OF DIAMONDS

rich men will not let their sons do the very thing
that made them great. As a rule, the rich man
will not allow his son to work—and his mother!
Why, she would think it was a social disgrace
if her poor, weak, little lily-fingered, sissy sort of
a boy had to earn his living with honest toil. I
have no pity for such rich men's sons.

I remember one at Niagara Falls. I think
I remember one a great deal nearer. I think
there are gentlemen present who were at a great
banquet, and I beg pardon of his friends. At a
banquet here in Philadelphia there sat beside me
a kind-hearted young man, and he said, "Mr.
Conwell, you have been sick for two or three years.
When you go out, take my limousine, and it will
take you up to your house on Broad Street."
I thanked him very much, and perhaps I ought
not to mention the incident in this way, but I
follow the facts. I got on to the seat with the
driver of that limousine, outside, and when we
were going up I asked the driver, "How much
did this limousine cost?" "Six thousand eight
hundred, and he had to pay the duty on it."
"Well," I said, "does the owner of this machine
ever drive it himself?" At that the chauffeur
laughed so heartily that he lost control of his machine. He was so surprised at the question that
he ran up on the sidewalk, and around a corner
lamp-post out into the street again. And when he
got out into the street he laughed till the whole
machine trembled. He said: "He drive this ma-

chine! Oh, he would be lucky if he knew enough to get out when we get there."

I must tell you about a rich man's son at Niagara Falls. I came in from the lecture to the hotel, and as I approached the desk of the clerk there stood a millionaire's son from New York. He was an indescribable specimen of anthropologic potency. He had a skull-cap on one side of his head, with a gold tassel in the top of it, and a gold-headed cane under his arm with more in it than in his head. It is a very difficult thing to describe that young man. He wore an eyeglass that he could not see through, patent-leather boots that he could not walk in, and pants that he could not sit down in—dressed like a grasshopper. This human cricket came up to the clerk's desk just as I entered, adjusted his unseeing eye-glass, and spake in this wise to the clerk. You see, he thought it was "Hinglish, you know," to lisp. "Thir, will you have the kindness to supply me with thome papah and enwelophs!" The hotel clerk measured that man quick, and he pulled the envelopes and paper out of a drawer, threw them across the counter toward the young man, and then turned away to his books. You should have seen that young man when those envelopes came across that counter. He swelled up like a gobbler turkey, adjusted his unseeing eye-glass, and yelled: "Come right back here. Now thir, will you order a thervant to take that papah and enwelophs to yondah dethk." Oh, the poor, miserable, contemptible American monkey! He could not carry paper and envelopes twenty feet. I suppose he could not get his arms down to do it. I have no pity for such travesties upon human nature. If you have not capital, young man, I am glad of it. What you need is common sense, not copper cents.

The best thing I can do is to illustrate by actual facts well-known to you all. A. T. Stewart, a poor boy in New York, had $1.50 to begin life on. He lost 87½ cents of that on the very first venture. How fortunate that young man who loses the first time he gambles. That boy said, "I will never gamble again in business," and he never did. How came he to lose 87½ cents? You probably all know the story how he lost it—because he bought some needles, threads, and buttons to sell which people did not want, and had them left on his hands, a dead loss. Said the boy, "I will not lose any more money in that way." Then he went around first to the doors and asked the people what they did want. Then when he had found out what they wanted he invested his 62½ cents to supply a known demand. Study it wherever you choose—in business, in your profession, in your housekeeping, whatever your life, that one thing is the secret of success. You must first know the demand. You must first know what people need, and then invest yourself where you are most needed. A. T. Stewart went on that principle until he was worth what amounted

ACRES OF DIAMONDS

afterward to forty millions of dollars, owning the very store in which Mr. Wanamaker carries on his great work in New York. His fortune was made by his losing something, which taught him the great lesson that he must only invest himself or his money in something that people need. When will you salesmen learn it? When will you manufacturers learn that you must know the changing needs of humanity if you would succeed in life? Apply yourselves, all you Christian people, as manufacturers or merchants or workmen to supply that human need. It is a great principle as broad as humanity and as deep as the Scripture itself.

The best illustration I ever heard was of John Jacob Astor. You know that he made the money of the Astor family when he lived in New York. He came across the sea in debt for his fare. But that poor boy with nothing in his pocket made the fortune of the Astor family on one principle. Some young man here to-night will say, "Well, they could make those fortunes over in New York, but they could not do it in Philadelphia!" My friends, did you ever read that wonderful book of Riis (his memory is sweet to us because of his recent death), wherein is given his statistical account of the records taken in 1889 of 107 millionaires of New York. If you read the account you will see that out of the 107 millionaires only seven made their money in New York. Out of the 107 millionaires worth ten million dollars

in real estate then, 67 of them made their money
in towns of less than 3,500 inhabitants. The
richest man in this country to-day, if you read
the real-estate values, has never moved away from
a town of 3,500 inhabitants. It makes not so
much difference where you are as who you are.
But if you cannot get rich in Philadelphia you
certainly cannot do it in New York.

Now John Jacob Astor illustrated what can
be done anywhere. He had a mortgage once on
a millinery-store, and they could not sell bonnets
enough to pay the interest on his money. So
he foreclosed that mortgage, took possession of
the store, and went into partnership with the very
same people, in the same store, with the same
capital. He did not give them a dollar of capital.
They had to sell goods to get any money. Then
he left them alone in the store just as they had
been before, and he went out and sat down on
a bench in the park in the shade. What was
John Jacob Astor doing out there, and in partnership with people who had failed on his own hands?
He had the most important and, to my mind, the
most pleasant part of that partnership on his
hands. For as John Jacob Astor sat on that bench
he was watching the ladies as they went by;
and where is the man who would not get rich at
that business? As he sat on the bench if a lady
passed him with her shoulders back and head
up, and looked straight to the front, as if she
did not care if all the world did gaze on her, then

' he studied her bonnet, and by the time it was out of sight he knew the shape of the frame, the color of the trimmings, and the crinklings in the feather. I sometimes try to describe a bonnet, but not always. I would not try to describe a modern bonnet. Where is the man that could describe one? This aggregation of all sorts of driftwood stuck on the back of the head, or the side of the neck, like a rooster with only one tail feather left. But in John Jacob Astor's day there was some art about the millinery business, and he went to the millinery-store and said to them: "Now put into the show-window just such a bonnet as I describe to you, because I have already seen a lady who likes such a bonnet. Don't make up any more until I come back." Then he went out and sat down again, and another lady passed him of a different form, of different complexion, with a different shape and color of bonnet. "Now," said he, "put such a bonnet as that in the show-window." He did not fill his show-window up-town with a lot of hats and bonnets to drive people away, and then sit on the back stairs and bawl because people went to Wanamaker's to trade. He did not have a hat or a bonnet in that show-window but what some lady liked before it was made up. The tide of custom began immediately to turn in, and that has been the foundation of the greatest store in New York in that line, and still exists as one of three stores. Its fortune was made by John Jacob Astor after they had failed in business, not by giving them any more money, but by finding out what the ladies liked for bonnets before they wasted any material in making them up. I tell you if a man could foresee the millinery business he could foresee anything under heaven!

Suppose I were to go through this audience to-night and ask you in this great manufacturing city if there are not opportunities to get rich in manufacturing. "Oh yes," some young man says, "there are opportunities here still if you build with some trust and if you have two or three millions of dollars to begin with as capital." Young man, the history of the breaking up of the trusts by that attack upon "big business" is only illustrating what is now the opportunity of the smaller man. The time never came in the history of the world when you could get rich so quickly manufacturing without capital as you can now.

But you will say, "You cannot do anything of the kind. You cannot start without capital." Young man, let me illustrate for a moment. I must do it. It is my duty to every young man and woman, because we are all going into business very soon on the same plan. Young man, remember if you know what people need you have gotten more knowledge of a fortune than any amount of capital can give you.

There was a poor man out of work living in Hingham, Massachusetts. He lounged around the house until one day his wife told him to get out and work, and, as he lived in Massachusetts, he obeyed his wife. He went out and sat down on the shore of the bay, and whittled a soaked shingle into a wooden chain. His children that evening quarreled over it, and he whittled a second one to keep peace. While he was whittling the second one a neighbor came in and said: "Why don't you whittle toys and sell them? You could make money at that." "Oh," he said, "I would not know what to make." "Why don't you ask your own children right here in your own house what to make?" "What is the use of trying that?" said the carpenter. "My children are different from other people's children." (I used to see people like that when I taught school.) But he acted upon the hint, and the next morning when Mary came down the stairway, he asked, "What do you want for a toy?" She began to tell him she would like a doll's bed, a doll's washstand, a doll's carriage, a little doll's umbrella, and went on with a list of things that would take him a lifetime to supply. So, consulting his own children, in his own house, he took the firewood, for he had no money to buy lumber, and whittled those strong, unpainted Hingham toys that were for so many years known all over the world. That man began to make those toys for his own children, and then made copies and sold them through the boot-and-shoe store next door. He began to make a little money, and then a little more, and Mr. Lawson, in his *Frenzied*

Finance says that man is the richest man in old Massachusetts, and I think it is the truth. And that man is worth a hundred millions of dollars to-day, and has been only thirty-four years making it on that one principle—that one must judge that what his own children like at home other people's children would like in their homes, too; to judge the human heart by oneself, by one's wife or by one's children. It is the royal road to success in manufacturing. "Oh," but you say, "didn't he have any capital?" Yes, a penknife, but I don't know that he had paid for that.

I spoke thus to an audience in New Britain, Connecticut, and a lady four seats back went home and tried to take off her collar, and the collar-button stuck in the buttonhole. She threw it out and said, "I am going to get up something better than that to put on collars." Her husband said: "After what Conwell said to-night, you see there is a need of an improved collar-fastener that is easier to handle. There is a human need; there is a great fortune. Now, then, get up a collar-button and get rich." He made fun of her, and consequently made fun of me, and that is one of the saddest things which comes over me like a deep cloud of midnight sometimes—although I have worked so hard for more than half a century, yet how little I have ever really done. Notwithstanding the greatness and the handsomeness of your compliment to-night, I do not believe there is one in ten of you that is going to make a million of dollars because you are here to-night; but it is not my fault, it is yours. I say that sincerely. What is the use of my talking if people never do what I advise them to do? When her husband ridiculed her, she made up her mind she would make a better collar-button, and when a woman makes up her mind "she will," and does not say anything about it, she does it. It was that New England woman who invented the snap button which you can find anywhere now. It was first a collar-button with a spring cap attached to the outer side. Any of you who wear modern waterproofs know the button that simply pushes together, and when you unbutton it you simply pull it apart. That is the button to which I refer, and which she invented. She afterward invented several other buttons, and then invested in more, and then was taken into partnership with great factories. Now that woman goes over the sea every summer in her private steamship—yes, and takes her husband with her! If her husband were to die, she would have money enough left now to buy a foreign duke or count or some such title as that at the latest quotations.

Now what is my lesson in that incident? It is this: I told her then, though I did not know her, what I now say to you, "Your wealth is too near to you. You are looking right over it"; and she had to look over it because it was right under her chin.

I have read in the newspaper that a woman

never invented anything. Well, that newspaper ought to begin again. Of course, I do not refer to gossip—I refer to machines—and if I did I might better include the men. That newspaper could never appear if women had not invented something. Friends, think. Ye women, think! You say you cannot make a fortune because you are in some laundry, or running a sewing-machine, it may be, or walking before some loom, and yet you can be a millionaire if you will but follow this almost infallible direction.

When you say a woman doesn't invent anything, I ask, Who invented the Jacquard loom that wove every stitch you wear? Mrs. Jacquard. The printer's roller, the printing-press, were invented by farmers' wives. Who invented the cotton-gin of the South that enriched our country so amazingly? Mrs. General Greene invented the cotton-gin and showed the idea to Mr. Whitney, and he, like a man, seized it. Who was it that invented the sewing-machine? If I would go to school tomorrow and ask your children they would say, "Elias Howe."

He was in the Civil War with me, and often in my tent, and I often heard him say that he worked fourteen years to get up that sewing-machine. But his wife made up her mind one day that they would starve to death if there wasn't something or other invented pretty soon, and so in two hours she invented the sewing-machine. Of course he took out the patent in his name. Men always do that. Who was it that invented the mower and the reaper? According to Mr. McCormick's confidential communication, so recently published, it was a West Virginia woman, who, after his father and he had failed altogether in making a reaper and gave it up, took a lot of shears and nailed them together on the edge of a board, with one shaft of each pair loose, and then wired them so that when she pulled the wire one way it closed them, and when she pulled the wire the other way it opened them, and there she had the principle of the mowing-machine. If you look at a mowing-machine, you will see it is nothing but a lot of shears. If a woman can invent a mowing-machine, if a woman can invent a Jacquard loom, if a woman can invent a cotton-gin, if a woman can invent a trolley switch—as she did and made the trolleys possible; if a woman can invent, as Mr. Carnegie said, the great iron squeezers that laid the foundation of all the steel millions of the United States, "we men" can invent anything under the stars! I say that for the encouragement of the men.

Who are the great inventors of the world? Again this lesson comes before us. The great inventor sits next to you, or you are the person yourself. "Oh," but you will say, "I have never invented anything in my life." Neither did the great inventors until they discovered one great secret. Do you think it is a man with a head like a bushel measure or a man like a stroke of lightning?

It is neither. The really great man is a plain, straightforward, every-day, common-sense man. You would not dream that he was a great inventor if you did not see something he had actually done. His neighbors do not regard him so great. You never see anything great over your back fence. You say there is no greatness among your neighbors. It is all away off somewhere else. Their greatness is ever so simple, so plain, so earnest, so practical, that the neighbors and friends never recognize it.

True greatness is often unrecognized. That is sure. You do not know anything about the greatest men and women. I went out to write the life of General Garfield, and a neighbor, knowing I was in a hurry, and as there was a great crowd around the front door, took me around to General Garfield's back door and shouted, "Jim! Jim!" And very soon "Jim" came to the door and let me in, and I wrote the biography of one of the grandest men of the nation, and yet he was just the same old "Jim" to his neighbor. If you know a great man in Philadelphia and you should meet him to-morrow, you would say, "How are you, Sam?" or "Good morning, Jim." Of course you would. That is just what you would do.

One of my soldiers in the Civil War had been sentenced to death, and I went up to the White House in Washington—sent there for the first time in my life—to see the President. I went into the waiting-room and sat down with a lot of others on the benches, and the secretary asked one after another to tell him what they wanted. After the secretary had been through the line, he went in, and then came back to the door and motioned for me. I went up to that anteroom, and the secretary said: "That is the President's door right over there. Just rap on it and go right in." I never was so taken aback, friends, in all my life, never. The secretary himself made it worse for me, because he had told me how to go in and then went out another door to the left and shut that. There I was, in the hallway by myself before the President of the United States of America's door. I had been on fields of battle, where the shells did sometimes shriek and the bullets did sometimes hit me, but I always wanted to run. I have no sympathy with the old man who says, "I would just as soon march up to the cannon's mouth as eat my dinner." I have no faith in a man who doesn't know enough to be afraid when he is being shot at. I never was so afraid when the shells came around us at Antietam as I was when I went into that room that day; but I finally mustered the courage— I don't know how I ever did—and at arm's-length tapped on the door. The man inside did not help me at all, but yelled out, "Come in and sit down!"

Well, I went in and sat down on the edge of a chair, and wished I were in Europe, and the man at the table did not look up. He was one of the world's greatest men, and was made great by one single rule. Oh, that all the young people of Philadelphia were before me now and I could say just this one thing, and that they would remember it. I would give a lifetime for the effect it would have on our city and on civilization. Abraham Lincoln's principle for greatness can be adopted by nearly all. This was his rule: Whatsoever he had to do at all, he put his whole mind into it and held it all there until that was all done. That makes men great almost anywhere. He stuck to those papers at that table and did not look up at me, and I sat there trembling. Finally, when he had put the string around his papers, he pushed them over to one side and looked over to me, and a smile came over his worn face. He said: "I am a very busy man and have only a few minutes to spare. Now tell me in the fewest words what it is you want." I began to tell him, and mentioned the case, and he said: "I have heard all about it and you do not need to say any more. Mr. Stanton was talking to me only a few days ago about that. You can go to the hotel and rest assured that the President never did sign an order to shoot a boy under twenty years of age, and never will. You can say that to his mother any-how."

Then he said to me, "How is it going in the field?" I said, "We sometimes get discouraged." And he said: "It is all right. We are going to win out now. We are getting very near the light. No man ought to wish to be President of the United States, and I will be glad when I get through; then Tad and I are going out to Springfield, Illinois. I have bought a farm out there and I don't care if I again earn only twenty-five cents a day. Tad has a mule team, and we are going to plant onions."

Then he asked me, "Were you brought up on a farm?" I said, "Yes; in the Berkshire Hills of Massachusetts." He then threw his leg over the corner of the big chair and said, "I have heard many a time, ever since I was young, that up there in those hills you have to sharpen the noses of the sheep in order to get down to the grass between the rocks." He was so familiar, so everyday, so farmer-like, that I felt right at home with him at once.

He then took hold of another roll of paper, and looked up at me and said, "Good morning." I took the hint then and got up and went out. After I had gotten out I could not realize I had seen the President of the United States at all. But a few days later, when still in the city, I saw the crowd pass through the East Room by the coffin of Abraham Lincoln, and when I looked at the upturned face of the murdered President I felt then that the man I had seen such a short time before, who, so simple a man, so plain a man, was one of the greatest men that God ever raised up to lead a nation on to ultimate liberty.

ACRES OF DIAMONDS

Yet he was only "Old Abe" to his neighbors. When they had the second funeral, I was invited among others, and went out to see that same coffin put back in the tomb at Springfield. Around the tomb stood Lincoln's old neighbors, to whom he was just "Old Abe." Of course that is all they would say.

Did you ever see a man who struts around altogether too large to notice an ordinary working mechanic? Do you think he is great? He is nothing but a puffed-up balloon, held down by his big feet. There is no greatness there.

Who are the great men and women? My attention was called the other day to the history of a very little thing that made the fortune of a very poor man. It was an awful thing, and yet because of that experience he—not a great inventor or genius—invented the pin that now is called the safety-pin, and out of that safety-pin made the fortune of one of the great aristocratic families of this nation.

A poor man in Massachusetts who had worked in the nail-works was injured at thirty-eight, and he could earn but little money. He was employed in the office to rub out the marks on the bills made by pencil memorandums, and he used a rubber until his hand grew tired. He then tied a piece of rubber on the end of a stick and worked it like a plane. His little girl came and said, "Why, you have a patent, haven't you?" The father said afterward, "My daughter told me when I took that stick and put the rubber on the end that there was a patent, and that was the first thought of that." He went to Boston and applied for his patent, and every one of you that has a rubber-tipped pencil in your pocket is now paying tribute to the millionaire. No capital, not a penny did he invest in it. All was income, all the way up into the millions.

But let me hasten to one other greater thought. "Show me the great men and women who live in Philadelphia." A gentleman over there will get up and say: "We don't have any great men in Philadelphia. They don't live here. They live away off in Rome or St. Petersburg or London or Manayunk, or anywhere else but here in our town." I have come now to the apex of my thought. I have come now to the heart of the whole matter and to the center of my struggle: Why isn't Philadelphia a greater city in its greater wealth? Why does New York excel Philadelphia? People say, "Because of her harbor." Why do many other cities of the United States get ahead of Philadelphia now? There is only one answer, and that is because our own people talk down their own city. If there ever was a community on earth that has to be forced ahead, it is the city of Philadelphia. If we are to have a boulevard, talk it down; if we are going to have better schools, talk them down; if you wish to have wise legislation, talk it down; talk all the proposed improvements down. That is the only great wrong that I can lay at the feet of the magnificent Philadelphia that has been so universally kind to me. I say it is time we turn around in our city and begin to talk up the things that are in our city, and begin to set them before the world as the people of Chicago, New York, St. Louis, and San Francisco do. Oh, if we only could get that spirit out among our people, that we can do things in Philadelphia and do them well!

Arise, ye millions of Philadelphians, trust in God and man, and believe in the great opportunities that are right here—not over in New York or Boston, but here—for business, for everything that is worth living for on earth. There was never an opportunity greater. Let us talk up our own city.

But there are two other young men here to-night, and that is all I will venture to say, because it is too late. One over there gets up and says, "There is going to be a great man in Philadelphia, but never was one." "Oh, is that so? When are you going to be great?" "When I am elected to some political office." Young man, won't you learn a lesson in the primer of politics that it is a *prima facie* evidence of littleness to hold office under our form of government? Great men get into office sometimes, but what this country needs is men that will do what we tell them to do. This nation—where the people rule—is governed by the people, for the people, and so long as it is, then the office-holder is but the servant of the people, and the Bible says the servant cannot be greater than the master. The Bible says, "He that is sent cannot be greater than Him who sent Him." The people rule, or should rule, and if they do, we do not need the greater men in office. If the great men in America took our offices, we would change to an empire in the next ten years.

I know of a great many young women, now that woman's suffrage is coming, who say, "I am going to be President of the United States some day." I believe in woman's suffrage, and there is no doubt but what it is coming, and I am getting out of the way, anyhow. I may want an office by and by myself; but if the ambition for an office influences the women in their desire to vote, I want to say right here what I say to the young men, that if you only get the privilege of casting one vote, you don't get anything that is worth while. Unless you can control more than one vote, you will be unknown, and your influence so dissipated as practically not to be felt. This country is not run by votes. Do you think it is? It is governed by influence. It is governed by the ambitions and the enterprises which control votes. The young woman that thinks she is going to vote for the sake of holding an office is making an awful blunder.

That other young man gets up and says, "There are going to be great men in this country and in Philadelphia." "Is that so? When?" "When there comes a great war, when we get into difficulty through watchful waiting in Mexico; when we get into war with England over some frivolous deed, or with Japan or China or New Jersey or some distant country. Then I will march up to the cannon's mouth; I will sweep up among the glistening bayonets; I will leap into the arena and tear down the flag and bear it away in triumph. I will come home with stars on my shoulder, and hold every office in the gift of the nation, and I will be great." No, you won't. You think you are going to be made great by an office, but remember that if you are not great before you get the office, you won't be great when you secure it. It will only be a burlesque in that shape.

We had a Peace Jubilee here after the Spanish War. Out West they don't believe this, because they said, "Philadelphia would not have heard of any Spanish War until fifty years hence." Some of you saw the procession go up Broad Street. I was away, but the family wrote to me that the tally-ho coach with Lieutenant Hobson upon it stopped right at the front door and the people shouted, "Hurrah for Hobson!" and if I had been there I would have yelled too, because he deserves much more of his country than he has ever received. But suppose I go into school and say, "Who sunk the *Merrimac* at Santiago?" and if the boys answer me, "Hobson," they will tell me seven-eighths of a lie. There were seven other heroes on that steamer, and they, by virtue of their position, were continually exposed to the

ACRES OF DIAMONDS

Spanish fire, while Hobson, as an officer, might reasonably be behind the smoke-stack. You have gathered in this house your most intelligent people, and yet, perhaps, not one here can name the other seven men.

We ought not to so teach history. We ought to teach that, however humble a man's station may be, if he does his full duty in that place he is just as much entitled to the American people's honor as is the king upon his throne. But we do not so teach. We are now teaching everywhere that the generals do all the fighting.

I remember that, after the war, I went down to see General Robert E. Lee, that magnificent Christian gentleman of whom both North and South are now proud as one of our great Americans. The general told me about his servant, "Rastus," who was an enlisted colored soldier. He called him in one day to make fun of him, and said, "Rastus, I hear that all the rest of your company are killed, and why are you not killed?" Rastus winked at him and said, "'Cause when there is any fightin' goin' on I stay back with the generals."

I remember another illustration. I would leave it out but for the fact that when you go to the library to read this lecture, you will find this has been printed in it for twenty-five years. I shut my eyes—shut them close—and lo! I see the faces of my youth. Yes, they sometimes say to me, "Your hair is not white; you are working night and day without seeming ever to stop; you can't be old." But when I shut my eyes, like any other man of my years, oh, then come trooping back the faces of the loved and lost of long ago, and I know, whatever men may say, it is evening-time.

I shut my eyes now and look back to my native town in Massachusetts, and I see the cattle-show ground on the mountain-top; I can see the horse-sheds there. I can see the Congregational church; see the town hall and mountaineers' cottages; see a great assembly of people turning out, dressed resplendently, and I can see flags flying and hand-kerchiefs waving and hear bands playing. I can see that company of soldiers that had re-enlisted marching up on that cattle-show ground. I was but a boy, but I was captain of that company and puffed out with pride. A cambric needle would have burst me all to pieces. Then I thought it was the greatest event that ever came to man on earth. If you have ever thought you would like to be a king or queen, you go and be received by the mayor.

The bands played, and all the people turned out to receive us. I marched up that Common so proud at the head of my troops, and we turned down into the town hall. Then they seated my soldiers down the center aisle and I sat down on the front seat. A great assembly of people—a hundred or two—came in to fill the town hall, so that they stood up all around. Then the town officers came in and formed a half-circle. The mayor of the town sat in the middle of the platform. He was a man who had never held office before; but he was a good man, and his friends have told me that I might use this without giving them offense. He was a good man, but he thought an office made a man great. He came up and took his seat, adjusted his powerful spectacles, and looked around, when he suddenly spied me sitting there on the front seat. He came right forward on the platform and invited me up to sit with the town officers. No town officer ever took any notice of me before I went to war, except to advise the teacher to thrash me, and now I was invited up on the stand with the town officers. Oh my! the town mayor was then the emperor, the king of our day and our time. As I came up on the platform they gave me a chair about this far, I would say, from the front.

When I had got seated, the chairman of the Selectmen arose and came forward to the table, and we all supposed he would introduce the Congregational minister, who was the only orator in town, and that he would give the oration to the returning soldiers. But, friends, you should have seen the surprise which ran over the audience when they discovered that the old fellow was going to deliver that speech himself. He had never made a speech in his life, but he fell into the same error that hundreds of other men have fallen into. It seems so strange that a man won't learn he must speak his piece as a boy if he intends to be an orator when he is grown, but he seems to think all he has to do is to hold an office to be a great orator.

So he came up to the front, and brought with him a speech which he had learned by heart walking up and down the pasture, where he had frightened the cattle. He brought the manuscript with him and spread it out on the table so as to be sure he might see it. He adjusted his spectacles and leaned over it for a moment and marched back on that platform, and then came forward like this—tramp, tramp, tramp. He must have studied the subject a great deal, when you come to think of it, because he assumed an "elocutionary" attitude. He rested heavily upon his left heel, threw back his shoulders, slightly advanced the right foot, opened the organs of speech, and advanced his right foot at an angle of forty-five. As he stood in that elocutionary attitude, friends, this is just the way that speech went. Some people say to me, "Don't you exaggerate?" That would be impossible. But I am here for the lesson and not for the story, and this is the way it went:

"Fellow-citizens—" As soon as he heard his voice his fingers began to go like that, his knees began to shake, and then he trembled all over. He choked and swallowed and came around to the table to look at the manuscript. Then he gathered himself up with clenched fists and came back: "Fellow-citizens, we are— Fellow-citizens, we are—we are—we are—we are—we are—we are very happy—we are very happy—we are very happy. We are very happy to welcome back to their native town these soldiers who have fought and bled—and come back again to their native town. We are especially—we are especially—we are especially. We are especially pleased to see with us to-day this young hero" (that meant me)—"this young hero who in imagination" (friends, remember he said that; if he had not said "in imagination" I would not be egotistic enough to refer to it at all)—"this young hero who in imagination we have seen leading—we have seen leading—leading. We have seen leading his troops on to the deadly breach. We have seen his shining—we have seen his shining—his shining—his shining sword—flashing. Flashing in the sunlight, as he shouted to his troops, 'Come on'!"

Oh dear, dear, dear! how little that good man knew about war. If he had known anything about war at all he ought to have known what any of my G. A. R. comrades here to-night will tell you is true, that it is next to a crime for an officer of infantry ever in time of danger to go ahead of his men. "I, with my shining sword flashing in the sunlight, shouting to my troops, 'Come on'!" I never did it. Do you suppose I would get in front of my men to be shot in front by the enemy and in the back by my own men? That is no place for an officer. The place for the officer in actual battle is behind the line. How often, as a staff officer, I rode down the line, when our men were suddenly called to the line of battle, and the Rebel yells were coming out of the woods, and shouted: "Officers to the rear! Officers to the rear!" Then every officer gets behind the line of private soldiers, and the higher the officer's rank the farther behind he goes. Not because he is any the less brave, but because the laws of war require that. And yet he shouted, "I, with my shining sword—" In that house there sat the company of my soldiers who had carried that boy across the Carolina rivers that he might not wet his feet. Some of them had gone far out to get a pig or a chicken. Some of them had gone to death under the shell-swept pines in the mountains of Tennessee, yet in the good man's speech they were scarcely known. He did refer to them, but only incidentally. The hero of the hour was this boy. Did the nation owe him anything? No, nothing then and nothing now. Why was he the hero? Simply because that man fell into that same human error—that this boy was great because he was an officer and these were only private soldiers.

Oh, I learned the lesson then that I will never forget so long as the tongue of the bell of time continues to swing for me. Greatness consists not in the holding of some future office, but really consists in doing great deeds with little means and the accomplishment of vast purposes from the private ranks of life. To be great at all one must be great here, now, in Philadelphia. He who can give to this city better streets and better sidewalks, better schools and more colleges, more happiness and more civilization, more of God, he will be great anywhere. Let every man or woman here, if you never hear me again, remember this, that if you wish to be great at all, you must begin where you are and what you are, in Philadelphia, now. He that can give to his city any blessing, he who can be a good citizen while he lives here, he that can make better homes, he that can be a blessing whether he works in the shop or sits behind the counter or keeps house, whatever be his life, he who would be great anywhere must first be great in his own Philadelphia.

FIFTY YEARS ON THE LECTURE PLATFORM

BY

RUSSELL H. CONWELL

AN Autobiography! What an absurd request! If all the conditions were favorable, the story of my public life could not be made interesting. It does not seem possible that any will care to read so plain and uneventful a tale. I see nothing in it for boasting, nor much that could be helpful. Then I never saved a scrap of paper intentionally concerning my work to which I could refer, not a book, not a sermon, not a lecture, not a newspaper notice or account, not a magazine article, not one of the kind biographies written from time to time by noble friends have I ever kept even as a souvenir, although some of them may be in my library. I have ever felt that the writers concerning my life were too generous and that my own work was too hastily done. Hence I have nothing upon which to base an autobiographical account, except the recollections which come to an overburdened mind.

My general view of half a century on the lecture platform brings to me precious and beautiful memories, and fills my soul with devout gratitude for the blessings and kindnesses which have been given to me so far beyond my deserts. So much more success has come to my hands than I ever expected; so much more of good have I found than even youth's wildest dream included; so much more effective have been my weakest endeavors than I ever planned or hoped— that a biography written truthfully would be mostly an account of what men and women have done for me.

I have lived to see accomplished far more than my highest ambition included, and have seen the enterprises I have undertaken rush by me, pushed on by a thousand strong hands until they have left me far behind them. The realities are like dreams to me. Blessings on the loving hearts and noble minds who have been so willing to sacrifice for others' good and to think only of what they could do, and never of what they should get! Many of them have ascended into the Shining Land, and here I am in mine age gazing up alone,

> *Only waiting till the shadows*
> *Are a little longer grown.*

Fifty years! I was a young man, not yet of age, when I delivered my first platform lecture. The Civil War of 1861-65 drew on with all its passions, patriotism, horrors, and fears, and I was studying law at Yale University. I had from childhood felt that I was "called to the ministry." The earliest event of memory is the prayer of my father at family prayers in the little old cottage in the Hampshire highlands of the Berkshire Hills, calling on God with a sobbing voice to lead me into some special service for the Saviour. It filled me with awe, dread, and fear, and I recoiled from the thought, until I determined to fight against it with all my power. So I sought for other professions and for decent excuses for being anything but a preacher.

Yet while I was nervous and timid before the class in declamation and dreaded to face any kind of an audience, I felt in my soul a strange impulsion toward public speaking which for years made me miserable. The war and the public meetings for recruiting soldiers furnished an outlet for my suppressed sense of duty, and my first lecture was on the "Lessons of History" as applied to the campaigns against the Confederacy.

That matchless temperance orator and loving friend, John B. Gough, introduced me to the little audience in Westfield, Massachusetts, in 1862. What a foolish little school-boy speech it must have been! But Mr. Gough's kind words of praise, the bouquets and the applause, made me feel that somehow the way to public oratory would not be so hard as I had feared.

From that time I acted on Mr. Gough's advice and "sought practice" by accepting almost every invitation I received to speak on any kind of a subject. There were many sad failures and tears, but it was a restful compromise with my conscience concerning the ministry, and it pleased my friends. I addressed picnics, Sunday - schools, patriotic meetings, funerals, anniversaries, commencements,

debates, cattle-shows, and sewing-circles without
partiality and without price. For the first five
years the income was all experience. Then vol-
untary gifts began to come occasionally in the
shape of a jack-knife, a ham, a book, and the
first cash remuneration was from a farmers' club,
of seventy-five cents toward the "horse hire."
It was a curious fact that one member of that
club afterward moved to Salt Lake City and was
a member of the committee at the Mormon
Tabernacle in 1872 which, when I was a corre-
spondent, on a journey around the world, employed
me to lecture on "Men of the Mountains" in the
Mormon Tabernacle, at a fee of five hundred dollars.

While I was gaining practice in the first years
of platform work, I had the good fortune to have
profitable employment as a soldier, or as a cor-
respondent or lawyer, or as an editor or as a
preacher, which enabled me to pay my own ex-
penses, and it has been seldom in the fifty years
that I have ever taken a fee for my personal use.
In the last thirty-six years I have dedicated
solemnly all the lecture income to benevolent
enterprises. If I am antiquated enough for an
autobiography, perhaps I may be aged enough to
avoid the criticism of being an egotist, when I
state that some years I delivered one lecture,
"Acres of Diamonds," over two hundred times
each year, at an average income of about one hundred and fifty dollars for each lecture.

ON THE PLATFORM

It was a remarkable good fortune which came to me as a lecturer when Mr. James Redpath organized the first lecture bureau ever established. Mr. Redpath was the biographer of John Brown of Harper's Ferry renown, and as Mr. Brown had been long a friend of my father's I found employment, while a student on vacation, in selling that life of John Brown. That acquaintance with Mr. Redpath was maintained until Mr. Redpath's death. To General Charles H. Taylor, with whom I was employed for a time as reporter for the Boston *Daily Traveler*, I was indebted for many acts of self-sacrificing friendship which soften my soul as I recall them. He did me the greatest kindness when he suggested my name to Mr. Redpath as one who could "fill in the vacancies in the smaller towns" where the "great lights could not always be secured."

What a glorious galaxy of great names that original list of Redpath lecturers contained! Henry Ward Beecher, John B. Gough, Senator Charles Sumner, Theodore Tilton, Wendell Phillips, Mrs. Mary A. Livermore, Bayard Taylor, Ralph Waldo Emerson, with many of the great preachers, musicians, and writers of that remarkable era. Even Dr. Holmes, John Whittier, Henry W. Longfellow, John Lothrop Motley, George William Curtis, and General Burnside were persuaded to appear one or more times, although they refused to receive pay. I cannot forget how ashamed I felt when my name appeared in the shadow of such names, and how sure I was that every acquaintance was ridiculing me behind my back. Mr. Bayard Taylor, however, wrote me from the *Tribune* office a kind note saying that he was glad to see me "on the road to great usefulness." Governor Clafflin, of Massachusetts, took the time to send me a note of congratulation. General Benjamin F. Butler, however, advised me to "stick to the last" and be a good lawyer.

The work of lecturing was always a task and a duty. I do not feel now that I ever sought to be an entertainer. I am sure I would have been an utter failure but for the feeling that I must preach some gospel truth in my lectures and do at least that much toward that ever-persistent "call of God." When I entered the ministry (1879) I had become so associated with the lecture platform in America and England that I could not feel justified in abandoning so great a field of usefulness.

The experiences of all our successful lecturers are probably nearly alike. The way is not always smooth. But the hard roads, the poor hotels, the late trains, the cold halls, the hot church auditoriums, the overkindness of hospitable committees, and the broken hours of sleep are annoyances one soon forgets; and the hosts of intelligent faces, the messages of thanks, and the effects of the earnings on the lives of young college men can never cease to be a daily joy. God bless them all.

ON THE PLATFORM

Often have I been asked if I did not, in fifty years of travel in all sorts of conveyances, meet with accidents. It is a marvel to me that no such event ever brought me harm. In a continuous period of over twenty-seven years I delivered about two lectures in every three days, yet I did not miss a single engagement. Sometimes I had to hire a special train, but I reached the town on time, with only a rare exception, and then I was but a few minutes late. Accidents have preceded and followed me on trains and boats, and were sometimes in sight, but I was preserved without injury through all the years. In the Johnstown flood region I saw a bridge go out behind our train. I was once on a derelict steamer on the Atlantic for twenty-six days. At another time a man was killed in the berth of a sleeper I had left half an hour before. Often have I felt the train leave the track, but no one was killed. Robbers have several times threatened my life, but all came out without loss to me. God and man have ever been patient with me.

Yet this period of lecturing has been, after all, a side issue. The Temple, and its church, in Philadelphia, which, when its membership was less than three thousand members, for so many years contributed through its membership over sixty thousand dollars a year for the uplift of humanity, has made life a continual surprise; while the Samaritan Hospital's amazing growth, and the Garretson Hospital's dispensaries, have been so continually ministering to the sick and poor, and have done such skilful work for the tens of thousands who ask for their help each year, that I have been made happy while away lecturing by the feeling that each hour and minute they were faithfully doing good. Temple University, which was founded only twenty-seven years ago, has already sent out into a higher income and nobler life nearly a hundred thousand young men and women who could not probably have obtained an education in any other institution. The faithful, self-sacrificing faculty, now numbering two hundred and fifty-three professors, have done the real work. For that I can claim but little credit; and I mention the University here only to show that my "fifty years on the lecture platform" has necessarily been a side line of work.

My best-known lecture, "Acres of Diamonds," was a mere accidental address, at first given before a reunion of my old comrades of the Forty-sixth Massachusetts Regiment, which served in the Civil War and in which I was captain. I had no thought of giving the address again, and even after it began to be called for by lecture committees I did not dream that I should live to deliver it, as I now have done, almost five thousand times. "What is the secret of its popularity?" I could never explain to myself or others. I simply know that I always attempt to enthuse myself on each occasion with the idea that it is a special opportunity to do good, and I interest

ON THE PLATFORM

myself in each community and apply the general principles with local illustrations.

The hand which now holds this pen must in the natural course of events soon cease to gesture on the platform, and it is a sincere, prayerful hope that this book will go on into the years doing increasing good for the aid of my brothers and sisters in the human family.

RUSSELL H. CONWELL.

South Worthington, Mass.,
September 1, 1913.

THE END

Sun Books
Sun Publishing
Supplement B-4

———◉———

Booklist of these fine Authors:
James Allen
Christian D. Larson
Orison Swett Marden
Ralph Waldo Trine

———◉———

JAMES ALLEN TITLES

ABOVE LIFE'S TURMOIL by James Allen. True Happiness, Immortal Man, Overcoming of Self, Uses of Temptation, Basis of Action, Belief that Saves, Thought and Action, Your Mental Attitude, The Supreme Justice, Use of Reason, Self-Discipline, Resolution, Contentment in Activity, Pleasant Pastures of Peace, Etc. 163p. 5X8. Paperback. ISBN 0-89540-203-3.

ALL THESE THINGS ADDED by James Allen. Entering the Kingdom, Soul's Great Need, At Rest in the Kingdom, The Heavenly Life, Divine Center, Eternal Now, "Original Simplicity", The Might of Meekness, Perfect Love, Greatness and Goodness, and Heaven in the Heart, Etc. 192p. 5X8. Paperback. ISBN 0-89540-129-0.

AS A MAN THINKETH by James Allen. Thought and Character, Effect of Thought on Circumstances, Effect of Thought on Health and the Body, Thought and Purpose, The Thought-Factor in Achievement, Visions and Ideals, Serenity. 88p. 5X8. Paperback. ISBN 0-89540-136-3.

BYWAYS OF BLESSEDNESS by James Allen. Right Beginnings, Small Tasks and Duties, Transcending Difficulties, Hidden Sacrifices, Sympathy, Forgiveness, Seeing No Evil, Abiding Joy, Silentness, Solitude, Understanding the Simple Laws of Life, Happy Endings, Etc. 202p. 5X8. Paperback. ISBN 0-89540-202-5.

THE DIVINE COMPANION by James Allen. Truth as Awakener, Truth as Protector, Of Discipline and Purification, Of Purity of Heart, The First Prophecy- Called Awakening, The Fifth Prophecy- Called Transition, The Second Exhortation- Concerning Humility, Instruction Concerning the Great Reality, Discourse Concerning The Way of Truth, Self-Restraint, Etc. 152p. 5X8. Paperback. ISBN 0-89540-329-3.

EIGHT PILLARS OF PROSPERITY by James Allen. Discussion on Energy, Economy, Integrity, Systems, Sympathy, Sincerity, Impartiality, Self-reliance, and the Temple of Prosperity. 233p. 5X8. Paperback. ISBN 0-89540-201-7.

ENTERING THE KINGDOM by James Allen. The Soul's Great Need, The Competitive Laws and the Laws of Love, The Finding of a Principle, At Rest in the Kingdom, And All Things Added. 82p. 5X8. Paperback. ISBN 0-89540-226-2.

FOUNDATION STONES TO HAPPINESS AND SUCCESS by James Allen. Right Principles, Sound Methods, True Actions, True Speech, Equal Mindedness, Good Results. 53p. 5X8. Paperback. ISBN 0-89540-327-7.

FROM PASSION TO PEACE by James Allen. Passion, Aspiration, Temptation, Transmutation, Transcendence, Beatitude, Peace. 64p. 5X8. Paperback. ISBN 0-89540-077-4.

FROM POVERTY TO POWER by James Allen. The Path to Prosperity, Way Out of Undesirable Conditions, Silent Power of Thought, Controlling and Directing One's Forces, Secret of Health, Success, and Power, The Way of Peace, Power of Meditation, Self and Truth, Spiritual Power, Realization of Selfless Love, Entering into the Infinite, Perfect Peace, Etc. 184p. 5X8. Paperback. ISBN 0-89540-061-8.

THE HEAVENLY LIFE by James Allen. The Divine Center, The Eternal Now, "Original Simplicity", Unfailing Wisdom, Might of Meekness, The Righteous Man, Perfect Love, Perfect Freedom, Greatness and Goodness, Heaven in the Heart. 84p. 5X8. Paperback. ISBN 0-89540-227-0.

THE LIFE TRIUMPHANT by James Allen. Faith and Courage, Manliness and Sincerity, Energy and Power, Self-Control and Happiness, Simplicity and Freedom, Right-Thinking and Repose, Calmness and Resource, Insight and Nobility, Man and the Master, and Knowledge and Victory. 114p. 5X8. Paperback. ISBN 0-89540-125-8.

LIGHT ON LIFE'S DIFFICULTIES by James Allen. The Light that Leads to Perfect Peace, Law of Cause and Effect in Human Life, Values- Spiritual and Material, Adherence to Principle, Management of the Mind, Self-Control, Acts and their Consequences, Way of Wisdom, Individual Liberty, Blessing and Dignity of Work, Diversity of Creeds, War and Peace, Brotherhood of Man, Life's Sorrows, Life's Change, Etc. 137p. 5X8. Paperback. ISBN 0-89540-127-3.

MAN: KING OF MIND, BODY AND CIRCUMSTANCE by James Allen. Inner World of Thoughts, Outer World of Things, Habit: Its Slavery and Its Freedom, Bodily Conditions, Poverty, Man's Spiritual Dominion, Conquest: Not Resignation. 55p. 5X8. Paperback. ISBN 0-89540-212-2.

MEN AND SYSTEMS by James Allen. Men and Systems, Work, Wages, and Well-Being, The Survival of the Fittest as Divine Law, Justice in Evil, Justice and Love, Self-Protection- Animal, Human, and Divine, Aviation and the New Consciousness, The New Courage. 149p. 5X8. Paperback. ISBN 0-89540-326-9.

THE MASTERY OF DESTINY by James Allen. Deeds, Character and Destiny, Science of Self-Control, Cause and Effect in Human Conduct, Training of the Will, Thoroughness, Mind-Building and Life-Building, Cultivation of Concentration, Practice of Meditation, Power of Purpose, Joy of Accomplishment. 120p. 5X8. Paperback. ISBN 0-89540-209-2.

MEDITATIONS, A YEAR BOOK by James Allen. "James Allen may truly be called the Prophet of Meditation. In an age of strife, hurry, religious controversy, heated arguments, ritual and ceremony, he came with his message of Meditation, calling men away from the din and strife of tongues into the peaceful paths of stillness within their own souls, where 'the Light that lighteth every man that cometh into the world' ever burns steadily and surely for all who will turn their weary eyes from the strife without to the quiet within." Contains two quotes and a brief commentary for each day of the year. 366p. 5X8. Paperback. ISBN 0-89540-192-4.

MORNING AND EVENING THOUGHTS by James Allen. Contains a separate and brief paragraph for each morning and evening of the month. 71p. 5X8. Paperback. ISBN 0-89540-137-1.

OUT FROM THE HEART by James Allen. Heart and the Life, Nature of Power of Mind, Formation of Habit, Doing and Knowing, First Steps in the Higher Life, Mental Conditions and Their Effects, Exhortation. 54p. 5X8. Paperback. ISBN 0-89540-228-9.

THE SHINING GATEWAY by James Allen. The Shining Gateway of Meditation, Temptation, Regeneration, Actions and Motives, Morality and Religion, Memory, Repetition and Habit, Words and Wisdom, Truth Made Manifest, Spiritual Humility, Spiritual Strength, Etc. 58p. 5X8. Paperback. ISBN 0-89540-328-5.

THROUGH THE GATE OF GOOD by James Allen. The Gate and the Way, Law and the Prophets, The Yoke and the Burden, The Word and the Doer, The Vine and the Branches, Salvation this Day. 66p. 5X8. Paperback. ISBN 0-89540-216-5.

THE WAY OF PEACE by James Allen. The Power of Meditation, The Two Masters: Self and Truth, Spiritual Power, Realization of Selfless Love, Entering into the Infinite, Saints, Sages and Saviors, The Law of Service, Realization of Perfect Peace. 113p. 5X8. Paperback. ISBN 0-89540-229-7.

PERSONALITY: IT'S CULTIVATION AND POWER AND HOW TO ATTAIN by Lily L. Allen. Personality, Right Belief, Self-Knowledge, Intuition, Decision and Promptness, Self-Trust, Thoroughness, Manners, Physical Culture, Mental, Moral and Spiritual Culture, Introspection, Emancipation, Self-Development, Self-Control and Mental Poise, Liberty, Transformation, Balance, Meditation and Concentration. 170p. 5X8. Paperback. ISBN 0-89540-218-1.

CHRISTIAN D. LARSON

BRAINS AND HOW TO GET THEM by Christian D. Larson. Building the Brain, Making Every Brain Cell Active, Principles in Brain Building, Practical Methods in Brain Building, Vital Secrets in Brain Building, Special Brain Development, The Inner Secret, The Finer Forces, Subjective Concentration, Principle of Concentration, Development of Business Ability, Accumulation and Increase, Individual Advancement, The Genius of Invention, The Musical Prodigy, Talent and Genius in Art, Talent and Genius in Literature, Vital Essentials in Brain Building. 233p. 5X8. Paperback. ISBN 0-89540-382-X.

YOUR FORCES AND HOW TO USE THEM by Christian D. Larson. How We Govern the Forces We Possess, The Use of Mind in Pratical Action, Training the Subconscious for Special Results, How Man Becomes What He Thinks, He Can Who Thinks He Can, How We Secure What We Persistently Desire, Concentration and the Power of Suggestion, The Development of the Will, The Building of a Great Mind, How Character Determines Constructive Action, The Creative Forces in Man, Imagination and the Master Mind, Ect. 331p. 5X8. Paperback. ISBN 0-89540-380-3.

ORISON SWETT MARDEN

AMBITION AND SUCCESS by Orison Swett Marden. What is Ambition?, The Satisfied Man, The Influence of Environment, Unworthy Ambitions, Ambition Knows No Age Limit, Make Your Life Count, Visualize Yourself in a Better Position, Thwarted Ambition, Why Don't You Begin?. 75p. 5X8. Paperback. ISBN 0-89540-369-2.

BE GOOD TO YOURSELF by Orison Swett Marden. Be Good to Yourself, Where Does Your Energy Go?, The Strain to Keep Up Appearances, Nature as a Joy Builder, The Right to be Disagreeable, The Good Will Habit, Keeping a Level Head, Getting the Best Out of Employees, Don't Let Your Past Spoil Your Future, The Passion for Achievement, Neglect Your Business But Not Your Boy, The Home as a School of Good Manners, Self Improvement as Investment, Etc. 322p. 5X8. Paperback. ISBN 0-89540-364-1.

CHARACTER - The Grandest Thing in the World by Orison Swett Marden. A Grand Character, The Light Bearers, The Great-Hearted, Intrepidity of Spirit, "A Fragment of the Rock of Ages," Etc. 55p. 5X8. Paperback. ISBN 0-89540-297-1.

CHEERFULNESS AS A LIFE POWER by Orison Swett Marden. What Vanderbilt Paid for Twelve Laughs, The Cure for Americanitis, Oiling Your Business Machinery, Taking Your Fun Every Day as You Do Your Work, Finding What You Do Not Seek, "Looking Pleasant"- A Thing to be Worked From the Inside, The Sunshine Man. 79p. 5X8. Paperback. ISBN 0-89540-363-3.

EVERY MAN A KING or Might in Mind Mastery by Orison Swett Marden. Steering Thought Prevents Life Wrecks, How Mind Rules the Body, Thought Causes Health and Disease, Overcoming Fear, Mastering our Moods, The Power of Cheerful Thinking, Affirmation Creates Power, How Thinking Brings Success, Building Character, The Power of Imagination, How to Control Thought, Etc. 240p. 5X8. Paperback. ISBN 0-89540-334-X.

THE EXCEPTIONAL EMPLOYEE by Orison Swett Marden. The Exceptional Employee, Self-Discovery, Conquering an Uncongenial Environment, The Power of Enthusiasm, Self-Confidence Gets the Job, Why A Good Appearance Wins, Getting the Position That Calls Out Your Best, Health as Business Capital, Putting Your Best into Everything, In Cheating Your Employer You Cheat Yourself, Keeping Your Working Standards Up, Gray Hairs Seeking a Job, All Work and No Play a Bad Policy, Make Your Work Your Masterpiece, Etc. 202p. 5X8. Paperback. ISBN 0-89540-352-8.

GETTING ON by Orison Swett Marden. Who Holds You Down?, A Cheery Disposition, How to Be Popular, Physical Vigor And Achievement, Begin Right- Right Away, Emergencies- the Test of Ability, Go Into Business for Yourself, The Stimulus of Rebuffs, Gentleness Versus Bluster, The Miracle of Polite Persistency, Over-Sensitivness as a Barrier, The Tragedy of Carelessness, The Love of Excellence, A Vacation as an Investment, On Commercializing One's Ability, Mere Money-Making is Not Success, Etc. 325p. 5X8. Paperback. ISBN 0-89540-370-6.

GOOD MANNERS- A PASSPORT TO SUCCESS by Orison Swett Marden. The Home Training, Self-Respect, Self-Control, Tact, The Relation of Courtesy to a Business Career, Manners in Public Life, The Law of Kindness. 64p. 5X8. Paperback. ISBN 0-89540-366-8.

HE CAN WHO THINKS HE CAN by Orison Swett Marden. He Can Who Thinks He Can, Getting Aroused, Education by Absorption, Freedom at Any Cost, What the World Owes to Dreamers, The Spirit in Which You Work, Responsibility Develops Power, Stand for Something, Happy, If Not, Why? Originality, Sizing Up People, Getting Away From Poverty, Etc. 245p. 5X8. Paperback. ISBN 0-89540-346-3.

THE HOUR OF OPPORTUNITY by Orison Swett Marden. The Hour of Opportunity: Are You Ready For It? Self-Made or Never Made, Do Not Wait For Opportunity, Self-Training, Do You Know a Good Thing When You See It?, Every-Day Opportunities, The Executive Quality, What Is My Right Place, "I Never Asked Anything About It," The Power of Adaption, Focus Your Energies, Become a Specialist, The Inspiration of a Great Purpose, Etc. 72p. 5X8. Paperback. ISBN 0-89540-336-6.

HOW THEY SUCCEEDED by Orison Swett Marden. Marshall Field, Alexander G. Bell, Helen Gould, Philip D. Armour, Mary E. Proctor, John Wanamaker, Darius Ogden Mills, Lillian Nordica, John D. Rockefeller, Julia Ward Howe, Thomas A. Edison, Lew Wallace, Andrew Carnegie, John Burroughs, James Whitcomb Riley, Etc. 365p. 5X8. Paperback. ISBN 0-89540-345-5.

HOW TO GET WHAT YOU WANT by Orison Swett Marden. How to Get What You Want, Discouragement a Disease- How to Cure It, The Force that Moves Mountains, Faith and Drugs, How to Find Oneself, How to Attract Prosperity, Heart-to-Heart Talks With Yourself, Etc. 331p. 5X8. Paperback. ISBN 0-89540-335-8.

HOW TO SUCCEED or Stepping Stones to Fame and Fortune by Orison Swett Marden. Seize Your Opportunity, How Did He Begin?, What Shall I Do?, Foundation Stones, The Conquest of Obstacles, To Be Great- Concentrate, Thoroughness, Courage and Will Power, Guard Your Weak Point, Live Upward, Moral Sunshine, Hold Up Your Head, Books and Success, Etc. 332p. 5X8. Paperback. ISBN 0-89540-371-4.

AN IRON WILL by Orison Swett Marden. Training the Will, Mental Discipline, Conscious Power, Do You Believe in Yourself? Will Power in its Relation to Health and Disease, The Romance of Achievement Under Difficulties, Concentrated Energy, Staying Power, Persistent Purpose, Success Against Odds, Etc. 49p. 5X8. Paperback. ISBN 0-89540-283-1.

LITTLE VISITS WITH GREAT AMERICANS or Success Ideals and How to Attain Them, Vol. I. by Orison Swett Marden. Thomas Alva Edison, Andrew Carnegie, Marshall Field, John Wanamaker, Darius Ogden Mills, Cornelius Vanderbilt, Samuel Gompers, Theodore Roosevelt, Nelson A. Miles, Jacob Gould Shurman, James Witcomb Riley, Ella Wheeler Wilcox, Lew Wallace, Mrs. Burton Harrison, Edwin Austin Abbey, Alice Barber Stevens, Frederic Remington, Charles Dana Gibson. Etc. 352p. 5X8. Paperback. ISBN 0-89540-372-2.

LITTLE VISITS WITH GREAT AMERICANS or Success Ideals and How to Attain Them, Vol. II. by Orison Swett Marden. Frederick Burr Opper, Marshall P. Wilder, Richard Mansfield, John Philip Sousa, Helen Keller, John Burroughs, Helen Miller Gould, Nathan Strauss, Robert Collyer, Lillian Nordica, Etc. Canadians: Robert Laird Borden, S.N. Parent, Andrew G. Blair, Sir William C. VanHorne, Etc. 389p. 5X8. Paperback. ISBN 0-89540-373-0.

LITTLE VISITS WITH GREAT AMERICANS or Success Ideals and How to Attain Them, TWO VOLUME SET by Orison Swett Marden. 741p. 5X8. Paperback. ISBN 0-89540-374-9.

MAKING LIFE A MASTERPIECE by Orison Swett Marden. Making Life a Masterpiece, Practical Dreamers, Where Your Opportunity Is, The Triumph of Common Virtues, Masterfulness and Physical Vigor, Curing the Curse of Indecision, Unlocking Your Possibilities, The Will to Succeed, The Kingship of Self Control, Finding Your Place, The Secret of Happiness, Etc. 329p. 5X8. Paperback. ISBN 0-89540-365-X.

THE MIRACLE OF RIGHT THOUGHT by Orison Swett Marden. Working for One Thing and Expecting Something Else, Expect Great Things of Yourself, Self-Encouragement by Self-Suggestion, Change the Thought- Change the Man, The Paralysis of Fear, Getting in Tune, A New Way of Bringing Up Children, Training for Longevity, As A Man Thinketh, Etc. 339p. 5X8. Paperback. ISBN 0-89540-311-0.

THE OPTOMISTIC LIFE by Orison Swett Marden. The Power of Amiability, The Inner Life as Related to Outward Beauty, The Value of Friends, The Cost of an Explosive Temper, Learn to Expect a Great Deal of Life, Mental Power, If You Can Talk Well, Brevity and Directness, What Distinguishes Work From Drudgery, Keeping Fit for Work, Mastering Moods, Business Integrity, Wresting Triumph from Defeat, Freshness in Work, Don't Take Your Business Troubles Home, Let It Go, Etc. 316p. 5X8. Paperback. ISBN: 0-89540-351-X.

PEACE, POWER, AND PLENTY by Orison Swett Marden. The Power of the Mind to Compel the Body, Poverty a Mental Disease, The Law of Opulence, Character-Building and Health-Building During Sleep, Health Through Right Thinking, Imagination and

Health, How Suggestion Influences Health, Why Grow Old?, The Miracle of Self-Confidence, Self-Control vs the Explosive Passions, Good Cheer- God's Medicine, Etc. 323p. 5X8. Paperback. ISBN 0-89540-343-9.

THE POWER OF PERSONALITY by Orison Swett Marden. What a Good Appearance Will Do, The Essentials of a Good Appearance, Cleanliness and Morals, The Importance of Dress, "The Manners Make the Man," Hindering Habits, Shyness, Personal Magnetism. 86p. 5X8. Paperback. ISBN 0-89540-362-5.

PUSHING TO THE FRONT VOL I by Orison Swett Marden. Opportunities Where You Are, Possibilities in Spare Time, How Poor Boys and Girls Go to College, Your Opportunity Confronts You-What, Will You Do With It?, Choosing a Vocation, Concentrated Energy, The Triumph of Enthusiasm, Promptness, Appearance, Personality, Common Sense, Accuracy, Persistence, Success Under Difficulties, Observation and Self-Improvement, The Triumph of the Common Virtues, Etc. 432p. 5X8. Paperback. ISBN 0-89540-331-5.

PUSHING TO THE FRONT VOL II by Orison Swett Marden. The Man With an Idea, The Will and the Way, Work and Wait, The Might of Little Things, Expect Great Things of Yourself, Stand for Something, Habit: The Servant or The Master, The Power of Purity, The Power of Suggestion, The Conquest of Poverty, The Home as a School of Good Manners, Thrift, Why Some Succeed and Others Fail, Character is Power, Rich Without Money, Etc. 441p. 5X8. Paperback. ISBN 0-89540-332-3.

PUSHING TO THE FRONT, TWO VOL. SET by Orison Swett Marden. 873p. 5x8. Paperback. ISBN: 0-89540-333-1

RISING IN THE WORLD or ARCHITECTS OF FATE by Orison Swett Marden. Dare, The Will and the Way, Uses of Obstacles, Self-Help, Work and Wait, Rich Without Money, Opportunities Where You Are, The Might of Little Things, Choosing a Vocation, The Man With an Idea, The Curse of Idleness, Etc. 318p. 5X8. Paperback. ISBN 0-89540-375-7.

THE SECRET OF ACHIEVEMENT by Orison Swett Marden. Moral Sunshine, "Blessed Be Drudgery", Honesty- As Principle and As Policy, Habit: The Servant or The Master, Courage, Self-Control, & The School of Life, Decide, Tenacity of Purpose, The Art of Keeping Well, Purity is Power, Etc. 301p. 5X8. Paperback. ISBN 0-89540-337-4.

SELF-INVESTMENT by Orison Swett Marden. If You Can- Talk Well, Put Beauty into Your Life, Enjoying What Others Own, Personality as a Success Asset, How to Be a Social Success, The Miracle of Tact, "I Had a Friend," Ambition, Education by Reading, Discrimination in Reading, Reading- A Spur to Ambition, The Self-Improvement Habit- A Great Asset, The Raising of Values, Self-Improvement Through Public Speaking, What a Good Appearance Will Do, Self-Reliance, Mental Friends and Foes. 315p. 5X8. Paperback. ISBN 0-89540-376-5.

SELLING THINGS by Orison Swett Marden. The Man Who Can Sell Things, Training the Salesman, Making a Favorable Impression, The Selling Talk or "Presentation", How to Get Attention, Friend-Winner and Business-Getter, Sizing Up the Prospect, How Suggestion Helps in Selling, The Gentle Art of Persuasion, Closing the Deal, Enthusiasm, Meeting and Forestalling Objections, Finding Customers, When You are Discouraged, Know Your Goods, Character is Capital, Keeping Fit and Salesmanship, Etc. 276p. 5X8. Paperback. ISBN 0-89540-339-0.

SUCCESS, A BOOK OF IDEALS, HELPS, AND EXAMPLES FOR ALL DESIRING TO MAKE THE MOST OF LIFE by Orison Swett Marden. Enthusiasm, Education Doing Difficulties, The Game of the World, Misfit Occupations, Doing Everyting to a Finish, "Help Yourself Society," "I Will," Conduct as Fine Art, Character Building, Medicine for the Mind, "This One Thing I Do," "I Had a Friend," Ideals. 347p. 5X8. Paperback. ISBN: 0-89540-360-9.

SUCCESS NUGGETS by Orison Swett Marden. Does an Education Pay?, To Take the Drudgery Out of Your Occupation, Where Happiness is Found, Why He Was Not Promoted, Why They Are Poor, Why He Found Life Disappointing, If You Would Be Very, Very Popular, What the World Wants, Don't Wait for Your Opportunity-Make It, When is Success a Failure?, He Succeeded in Business but Failed as a Man Because..., Does a Vacation Pay?, What Message Does Your Success Bring?, The Time Will Come, Etc. 76p. 5X8. Paperback. ISBN: 0-89540-354-4.

THE VICTORIOUS ATTITUDE by Orison Swett Marden. The Victorious Attitude, "According to Thy Faith," Making Dreams Come True, Making Yourself a Prosperity Magnet, The Triumph of Health Ideals, How to Make the Brain Work for Us During Sleep, Preparing the Mind For Sleep, How to Stay Young, Our Oneness With Infinite Life, Etc. 358p. 5X8. Paperback. ISBN: 0-89540-353-6.

WHY GROW OLD? by Orison Swett Marden. Marden instructs his reader to "hold to youthful, buoyant thought" and keep the imagination alive and flexible. Recognizing that we may be slaves to our attitudes, this text encourages us to make as much of ourselves as possible and in doing so watch as our lives are prolonged. 30p. 5X8. Paperback. ISBN 0-89540-340-4.

WINNING OUT by Orison Swett Marden. Good Manners and Success, Learning to Hold Your Tounge, The Emperor Who Earned

His Own Shoe-Leather, The Boy Who Did Not Know What Time It Was, The Golconda Diamonds, Heroic Youth, The Story of the Little Red Violin, Gold Dust, Seven Hundred Books and the Farm Boy, Training for the Presidency, Send Us a Man Who Can Swim, Abraham Lincoln's Advice About Schooling, Where Does the Fun Come In?. Etc. 251p. 5X8. Paperback. ISBN 0-89540-377-3.

YOU CAN, BUT WILL YOU? by Orison Swett Marden. The Magic Mirror, The New Philosophy of Life, Connecting With the Power that Creates, You Can, But Will You?, How Do You Stand With Yourself?, The New Philosophy in Business, What Are You Thinking?, Facing Life the Right Way, How to Realize Your Ambition, The Open Door, Do You Carry Victory in Your Face? Etc. 338p. 5X8. Paperback. ISBN 0-89540-342-0.

THE YOUNG MAN ENTERING BUSINESS by Orison Swett Marden. Personal Capital and Choosing a Vocation, Avoid Misfit Occupations, Fixity of Purpose, When It Is Right to Change, Personal Appearance, Manners, Sensitivness and Success, The Power of Decision, The Value of Business Training, Promotion from Exceptional Work, The Timid Man and Self-Confidence, Born to Conquer, Getting to the Point, Looking Well an Keeping Well, Salesmanship, System and Order, Shall I Go Into Business for Myself?, Tact and the Art of Winning, People's Confidence, Other Men's Brains, The Art of Advertising, Keeping Up With the Times, Friendship and Success. Etc. 307p. 5X8. Paperback. ISBN 0-89540-378-1.

RALPH WALDO TRINE

CHARACTER BUILDING THOUGHT POWER by Ralph Waldo Trine. "Have we within our power to determine at all times what types of habits shall take form in our lives? In other words, is habit-forming, character-building, a matter of mere chance, or do we have it within our control?" 51p. 5X8. Paperback. ISBN 0-89540-251-3.

EVERY LIVING CREATURE or Heart Training Through the Animal World, by Ralph Waldo Trine. "The tender and humane passion in the human heart is too precious a quality to allow it to be hardened or effaced by practices such as we often indulge in." *Ralph Waldo Trine.* 50p. 5X8. Paperback. ISBN 0-89540-309-9.

THE GREATEST THING EVER KNOWN by Ralph Waldo Trine. The Greatest Thing Ever Known, Divine Energies in Every-Day Life, The Master's Great but Lost Gift, The Philosopher's Ripest Life Thought, Sustained in Peace and Safety Forever. 57p. 5X8. Paperback. ISBN 0-89540-274-2.

THE HIGHER POWERS OF MIND AND SPIRIT by Ralph Waldo Trine. The Silent, Subtle Building Forces of Mind and Spirit, Thought as a Force in Daily Living, The Divine Rule in the Mind and Heart, The Powerful Aid of the Mind in Rebuilding Body- How Body Helps Mind, Etc. 240p. 5X8. Paperback. ISBN 0-89540-278-5.

IN THE FIRE OF THE HEART by Ralph Waldo Trine. With the People: A Revelation, The Conditions that Hold among Us, As Time Deals with Nations, As to Government, A Great People's Movement, Public Utilities for the Public Good, Labour and Its Uniting Power, Agencies Whereby We Shall Secure the People's Greatest Good, The Great Nation, The Life of the Higher Beauty and Power. 336p. 5X8. Paperback. ISBN 0-89540-310-2.

IN THE HOLLOW OF HIS HAND by Ralph Waldo Trine. The Present Demand to Know the Truth, The Thought- The Existing Conditions- and theReligions of Jesus' Time, What Jesus Realized, Jesus' Own Statement of the Essence of Religion, Was the Church Sanctioned or Established by Jesus?, Our Debt to the Prophets of Israel, The Power- The Beauty- and the Sustaining Peace. 242p. 5X8. Paperback. ISBN 0-89540-358-7.

THE MAN WHO KNEW by Ralph Waldo Trine. The Power of Love, All is Well, That Superb Teaching of "Sin", He Teaches the Great Truth, When a Brave Man Chooses Death, Bigotry in Fear Condemns and Kills, Love the Law of Life, The Creative Power of Faith and Courage, Etc. 230p. 5X8. Paperback. ISBN 0-89540-267-X.

MY PHILOSOPHY AND MY RELIGION by Ralph Waldo Trine. This Place: Amid the Silence of the Centuries, With the Oldest Living Things, My Philosophy, My Religion, The Creed of the Open Road. 130p. 5X8. Paperback. ISBN 0-89540-349-8.

THE NEW ALIGNMENT OF LIFE by Ralph Waldo Trine. Science and Modern Research, The Modern Spiritual Revival, The Vitilising Power of the Master's Message, Modern Philosophic Thought, A Thinking's Man Religion, A Healthy Mind in a Healthy Body, The Mental Law of Habit. 228p. 5X8. Paperback. ISBN 0-89540-347-1.

ON THE OPEN ROAD by Ralph Waldo Trine. "To realize always clearly that thoughts are forces, that like creates like and like attracts like, and that to determine one's thinking therefore is to determine his life." 65p. 5X8. Paperback. ISBN 0-89540-252-1.

THIS MYSTICAL LIFE OF OURS A Book of Suggestive Thoughts for Each Week Through the Year by Ralph Waldo Trine. The Creative Power of Thought, The Laws of Attraction, Prosperity, and Habit-Forming, Faith and Prayer- Their Nature, Self-Mastery,

Thoughts are Forces, How We Attract Success or Failure, The Secret and Power of Love, Will- The Human and The Divine, The Secret of the Highest Power, Wisdom or Interior Illumination, How Mind Builds Body, Intuition: The Voice of the Soul, To Be at Peace, Etc! 190p. 5X8. Paperback. ISBN 0-89540-279-3.

THROUGH THE SUNLIT YEAR by Ralph Waldo Trine. A book of Suggestive Thoughts for each day of the year from the writings of Ralph Waldo Trine. 250p. 5X8. Paperback. ISBN 0-89540-350-1.

WHAT ALL THE WORLD'S A-SEEKING by Ralph Waldo Trine. The Principle, The Application, The Unfoldment, The Awakening, The Incoming, Character-Building Thought Power. 224p. 5X8. Paperback. ISBN 0-89540-359-5.

THE WINNING OF THE BEST by Ralph Waldo Trine. Which Way is Life Leaning?, The Creative Power of Thought, The Best Is the Life, The Power That Makes Us What We Are, A Basis of Philosophy and Religion, How We Will Win the Best. 100p. 5X8. Paperback. ISBN 0-89540-348-X.

ELBERT HUBBARD

A MESSAGE TO GARCIA and Other Essays by Elbert Hubbard. A Message to García, The Boy from Missouri Valley, Help Yourself by Helping the House. "He was of big service to me in telling me the things I knew, but which I did not know I knew, until he told me." *Thomas A. Edison.* 48p. 5X8. Paperback. ISBN 0-89540-305-6.

Please write for our *Religions, Oriental, and Western Mysticism Book Catalog,* and our *Motivational and Success Book Catalog* from Sun Publishing Co., P.O. Box 5588-B4, Santa Fe, NM 87502-5588 USA.

Visit our web site at http://www.sunbooks.com/

10 SEP 1997   B-SUPPI.PM5